T0062642

Creating Responsive Websites Using HTML5 and CSS3

A Perfect Reference for Web Designers

Varun Gor

Apress®

Creating Responsive Websites Using HTML5 and CSS3: A Perfect Reference for Web Designers

Varun Gor
Bengaluru, India

ISBN-13 (pbk): 978-1-4842-9782-7   ISBN-13 (electronic): 978-1-4842-9783-4
https://doi.org/10.1007/978-1-4842-9783-4

Managing Director, Apress Media LLC: Welmoed Spahr
Acquisitions Editor: Divya Modi
Development Editor: James Markham
Coordinating Editor: Divya Modi

Cover designed by eStudioCalamar

Cover image by Freepik (www.freepik.com)

Distributed to the book trade worldwide by Apress Media, LLC, 1 New York Plaza, New York, NY 10004, U.S.A. Phone 1-800-SPRINGER, fax (201) 348-4505, e-mail orders-ny@springer-sbm.com, or visit www.springeronline.com. Apress Media, LLC is a California LLC and the sole member (owner) is Springer Science + Business Media Finance Inc (SSBM Finance Inc). SSBM Finance Inc is a **Delaware** corporation.

For information on translations, please e-mail booktranslations@springernature.com; for reprint, paperback, or audio rights, please e-mail bookpermissions@springernature.com.

Apress titles may be purchased in bulk for academic, corporate, or promotional use. eBook versions and licenses are also available for most titles. For more information, reference our Print and eBook Bulk Sales web page at http://www.apress.com/bulk-sales.

Any source code or other supplementary material referenced by the author in this book is available to readers on GitHub (https://github.com/Apress). For more detailed information, please visit https://www.apress.com/gp/services/source-code.

Paper in this product is recyclable

This book is dedicated to all the hustlers who have started from ground zero, putting in effort day after day to progress and achieve their goals.
#KeepItUp #Hustlers #Achievers

Table of Contents

About the Author

Varun Gor has more than 14 years of experience creating websites using Java, HTML, CSS, and JavaScript technologies and has worked with major IT companies with global clienteles. Varun graduated with a degree in computer science from Visvesvaraya Technological University in 2007 and has been part of the corporate world ever since.

Alongside his innate nature to explore technology, Varun is interested in outdoor activities; he has been part of club cricket and played division 3 league matches, been on a night trek near Bengaluru, and explored the city (less city more food) on his bike. In addition, he enjoys binge-watching good movies and TV shows (recently on web series), and at times he disconnects himself from the world around him using a device named headphones. Recently he has been trying his hand at cooking (God save his family).

About the Technical Reviewer

 **Sourabh Mishra** is an entrepreneur, developer, speaker, author, corporate trainer, and animator. He is a Microsoft guy; he is passionate about Microsoft technologies and a true .NET warrior. Sourabh has loved computers from childhood and started his career when he was just 15 years old. His programming experience includes C/C++, ASP.NET, C#, VB.NET, WCF, SQL Server, Entity Framework, MVC, Web API, Azure, jQuery, Highcharts, and Angular. He is also an expert in computer graphics. Sourabh is the author of *Practical Highcharts with Angular*, published by Apress. Sourabh has been awarded a Most Valuable Professional (MVP) status. He has the zeal to learn new technologies, sharing his knowledge on several online community forums.

He is a founder of IECE Digital and Sourabh Mishra Notes, an online knowledge-sharing platform where one can learn new technologies easily and comfortably.

Acknowledgments

First I would like to acknowledge my mother, wife, and brother who supported me in this venture and believed that I could do something I never thought was possible for me. I also acknowledge the guidance of my mentors who have shaped my career in the field of IT.

I would also like to acknowledge the Apress team, particularly Divya Modi and Shonmirin P.A., who went through the trouble of chasing down every minute detail and helping me shape this book. This was a tough time for them, and this book would have not been possible without them.

A special acknowledgment goes to my two furry friends, Coco and Arlo. The way they light up the surroundings has made it easy for me (actually everyone) to complete this book.

CHAPTER 1

Introduction to Web Development

This chapter will cover why web development is needed in today's digital world, how web development is done, and which technologies are capable of creating world-class and high-performing websites. Web developers need to know how HTML and CSS work, which will be covered in depth. I will briefly explain HTML elements and page structure so you can understand how HTML and CSS work in conjunction to create websites. I will also explain the problem that CSS solves and how to write CSS code.

Need for Web Development

Web development has become an increasingly vital aspect of modern life. The Internet has become an essential part of our daily routine, from shopping and entertainment to social media and education. With the constant expansion of the digital world, the demand for web development has grown exponentially.

Web development refers to the creation and maintenance of websites, web applications, and other online platforms. It involves a wide range of skills, including programming languages, database management, and graphic design. Web developers work together to create websites that are user-friendly, visually appealing, and accessible to a broad audience.

© Varun Gor 2023
V. Gor, *Creating Responsive Websites Using HTML5 and CSS3*,
https://doi.org/10.1007/978-1-4842-9783-4_1

One of the most significant reasons why web development is so essential is the rise of e-commerce. With an increasing number of people who shop online, businesses are realizing the importance of having an online presence. Websites are now more than just a way to provide information about a company; they are a critical tool for generating revenue. A well-designed website can attract more customers, increase brand awareness, and ultimately boost sales.

Web development is also crucial for the education sector. With the growth of e-learning, schools and universities need to have online platforms that provide easy access to course materials, discussions, and online assessments. This allows for a more flexible learning experience, making education more accessible to students who may not be able to attend traditional classrooms.

Moreover, web development has become essential in the healthcare industry. With the COVID-19 pandemic, healthcare providers have had to shift to telemedicine and virtual consultations. The development of online platforms has been crucial in providing care to patients, enabling doctors to diagnose and treat patients remotely. There are many such examples where technology has served a better and convenient means of accomplishing our daily tasks.

In addition to the practical uses, web development has become an essential tool for communication and entertainment. Social media platforms, such as Facebook and Twitter, have become a significant part of our daily lives. These platforms rely heavily on web development to provide users with an engaging and user-friendly experience.

In conclusion, web development is crucial for our modern-day world. It has become an essential tool for businesses, education, healthcare, and communication. As the Internet continues to evolve, the demand for web development will only increase. With the right skills and tools, web developers can help create websites and online platforms that are both functional and visually appealing, making the Internet a better place for everyone. The next section explains which technologies you can use.

Technologies Used in Web Development

The technologies used in web development have evolved significantly over the years, with new frameworks, tools, and languages emerging to improve the performance, functionality, and user experience of websites. Here are some of the key technologies that have evolved in web development. This book will be focusing on HTML and CSS.

- *HTML*: Hypertext Markup Language (HTML) has been the backbone of web development since the early days of the Internet. HTML has evolved over time, with new versions introducing new elements and features that make it easier to create complex websites and applications.

- *CSS*: Cascading Style Sheets (CSS) is used to style and lay out web pages. CSS has evolved to include new features, such as flexboxes, grids, and animations, that make it easier to create sophisticated designs and interactive user experiences.

- *JavaScript*: JavaScript is a scripting language used to create interactive websites and applications. JavaScript has evolved significantly over the years, with new libraries and frameworks such as React, Vue, and Angular making it easier to create complex web applications.

- *Server-side languages*: Server-side languages such as PHP, Python, and Ruby on Rails are used to create dynamic web applications that interact with databases and other server-side components. These languages have evolved to become more efficient and scalable, enabling developers to build complex web applications.

- *Web APIs*: Web application programming interfaces (APIs) allow web developers to integrate with other web services and data sources. Web APIs have evolved to include new standards such as RESTful APIs, which provide a simple and flexible way to interact with web services.

- *Cloud computing*: Cloud computing has transformed web development by providing a scalable and flexible infrastructure for web applications. Cloud platforms such as AWS, Google Cloud, and Microsoft Azure allow developers to deploy and manage web applications with ease.

- *Progressive web apps*: Progressive web apps (PWAs) are web applications that provide a user experience similar to native apps. PWAs have evolved to include new features such as service workers, which allow web applications to work offline and provide push notifications.

- *Artificial intelligence*: Artificial intelligence (AI) is increasingly being used in web development to improve user experiences and provide new functionality. AI-powered chatbots, for example, can provide instant customer support, while machine learning algorithms can personalize content and improve search results.

In conclusion, web development is the process of creating websites and web applications that are accessible through the Internet. It involves various aspects such as front-end development, back-end development, and web design. Web development has come a long way since the early days of the Internet, with new technologies and frameworks emerging to improve performance, functionality, and user experience. HTML, CSS, JavaScript, server-side languages, web APIs, cloud computing, PWAs, and AI are some of the key technologies that have transformed web development. As the Internet continues to evolve, web development will continue to play an increasingly important role in shaping the digital landscape. With the growing demand for online services and the increasing complexity of web applications, web development is poised to remain an exciting and dynamic field for years to come.

How HTML Works in a Web Browser

HTML is the backbone of the modern Web. It is the standard markup language used to create web pages, and it provides a way for developers to structure content and define its meaning. However, HTML doesn't work exactly the same way on all web browsers, and understanding these differences is crucial for building websites that work well across different platforms.

Web browsers are software applications that retrieve and display web pages from the Internet. There are several popular web browsers available today, including Google Chrome, Mozilla Firefox, Apple Safari, and Microsoft Edge; older browsers include Opera and Netscape Navigator. Each browser has its own rendering engine, which is responsible for interpreting and displaying HTML code.

Figure 1-1 shows some HTML code.

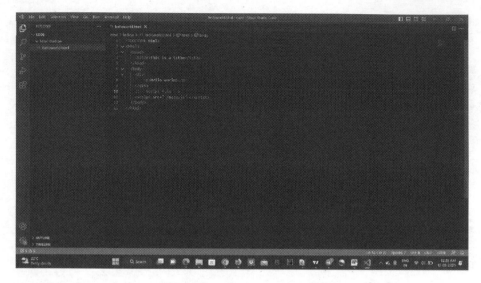

Figure 1-1. *Hello world HTML code*

The rendering engine is the part of the browser that takes the HTML, CSS, and JavaScript code and turns it into a visual representation on the screen. It parses the HTML and constructs a document object model (DOM), which is a treelike structure that represents the content and structure of the web page (Figure 1-2). The rendering engine then uses the DOM and CSS to determine how the web page should be displayed.

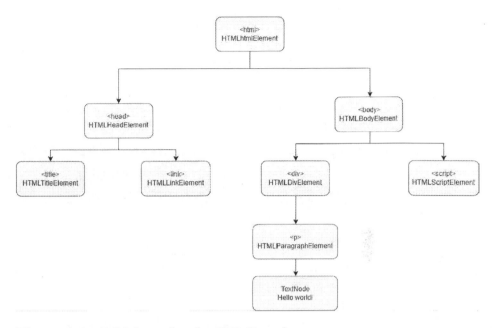

Figure 1-2. *DOM tree for the HTML code*

Different browsers have different rendering engines, which can lead to variations in how web pages are displayed. For example, some browsers may handle HTML and CSS in slightly different ways, leading to differences in layout and formatting. Additionally, different browsers may support different HTML features, which can impact how certain elements of a web page are displayed.

To ensure that web pages work well across different browsers, developers need to be aware of these differences and test their pages on multiple platforms. They can also use tools such as browser compatibility checkers to identify any issues that may arise when viewing their pages on different browsers.

In general, modern web browsers have good support for HTML5, which is the latest version of the HTML standard. This means developers can use the latest HTML features to create dynamic, interactive web pages that work well across different platforms.

Despite these efforts, however, there are still some differences in how HTML is interpreted and displayed across different browsers. These differences can be minor or significant, depending on the complexity of the web page and the specific features being used.

To overcome these differences, web developers can use a technique called *browser sniffing*, which involves detecting the specific browser being used and tailoring the HTML, CSS, and JavaScript code accordingly. However, this technique can be complex and may not always be reliable, so it's important for developers to stay up-to-date with the latest web standards and best practices.

HTML Elements

HTML elements are the building blocks of web pages, and they define the structure and content of the page. Each HTML element is surrounded by opening and closing tags, which tell the browser how to display the content. Though almost all of the tags have opening and closing tags, e.g., <tag_name></tag_name>, some tags have just the opening tag like <img>, <hr/>, etc. We are going to take a look at various HTML elements that are used to create web pages.

HTML elements can be categorized into several groups based on their function. Some of the most common categories include structural elements, text elements, multimedia elements, form elements, and scripting elements.

Structural Elements

Structural elements are used to define the overall structure of the web page. They include elements such as the <html>, <head>, <title>, and <body> tags. The <html> tag is used to define the document type, while the <head> tag contains information about the document, such as the title, author, and description. The <body> tag contains the main content of the web page.

Text Elements

Text elements are used to add text content to the web page. They include elements such as the <p>, <h1>–<h6>, and <em> tags. The <p> tag is used to create paragraphs, while the <h1>–<h6> tags are used to create headings of different sizes. The <em> tag is used to emphasize text, while the <strong> tag is used to highlight important text.

Here is an example of a heading tag:

```
<html>
    <body>
        <h1>This text is Heading 1.</h1>
        <h2>This text is Heading 2.</h2>
        <h3>This text is Heading 3.</h3>
        <h4>This text is Heading 4.</h4>
        <h5>This text is Heading 5.</h5>
        <h6>This text is Heading 6.</h6>
    </body>
</html>
```

Figure 1-3 shows an HTML file containing heading tag elements.

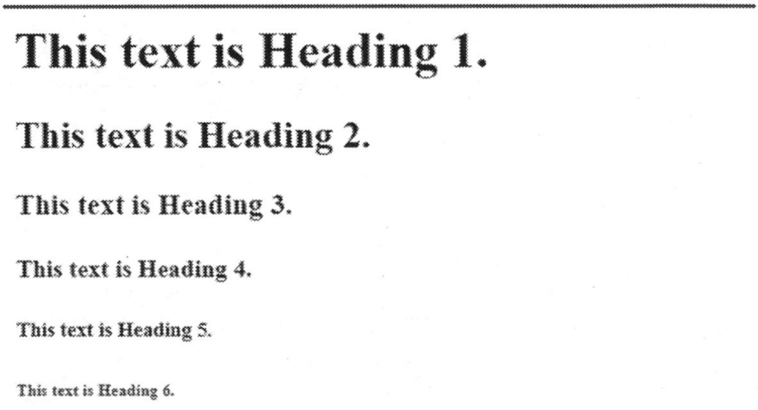

This text is Heading 1.

This text is Heading 2.

This text is Heading 3.

This text is Heading 4.

This text is Heading 5.

This text is Heading 6.

Figure 1-3. *HTML displaying how heading 1 to heading 6 is displayed in a browser*

Here is a code example of <p>:

```
<html>
    <body>
        <p>
            This paragraph is written inside &lt;p&gt; element.
            It will be displayed as continous text in the
            browser.
            Let us see how does it look on the browser.
        </p>
    </body>
</html>
```

Figure 1-4 shows how it looks in a browser.

Figure 1-4. *HTML rendering <p> element text in browser*

Multimedia Elements

Multimedia elements are used to add multimedia content to the web page, such as images and videos. They include elements such as the <img> and <video> tags. The <img> tag is used to display images, while the <video> tag is used to display videos.

Here is a code example for <img>:

```
<html>
    <body>
        <img src="../../../html dom.jpg" alt="dom image">
    </body>
</html>
```

Figure 1-5 shows how it looks in a browser.

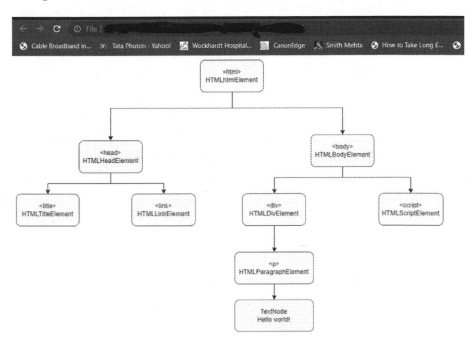

Figure 1-5. *HTML DOM structure*

Form Elements

Form elements are used to create forms on the web page, which allow users to input information. They include elements such as the <form>, <input>, and <button> tags. The <form> tag is used to create the form, while the <input> tag is used to create input fields for the user to enter information. The <button> tag is used to create buttons that the user can click to submit the form. We are going to take a deeper look at the form elements later in this book.

Scripting Elements

Scripting elements are used to add interactivity to the web page, such as animations and user interface elements. They include elements such as the <script> and <canvas> tags. The <script> tag is used to add JavaScript code to the web page, while the <canvas> tag is used to create graphics and animations. We will learn about scripts and animation in later chapters.

In addition to these categories, there are many other HTML elements that can be used to create web pages. Some of these elements are used for more specialized purposes, such as the <audio> tag for playing audio files or the <iframe> tag for embedding external web pages within the current page.

It's important to note that HTML elements are not the only component of a web page. Cascading Style Sheets and JavaScript are also used to define the visual appearance and interactivity of the page, respectively. However, HTML elements provide the foundation for the page and define its overall structure and content.

In conclusion, HTML elements are the building blocks of web pages. They define the structure and content of the page, and they are used to create everything from text to multimedia to forms and interactivity. By understanding the different types of HTML elements and how they are used, web developers can create rich and engaging web pages that are easy to navigate and interact with.

HTML Page Structure

An HTML page structure is composed of several different elements, each with its own purpose and function.

The Basic Structure of an HTML Page

An HTML page consists of several different parts, including the doctype, the head, and the body. The doctype is the first element in the page and tells the browser what version of HTML is being used. The head element contains information about the page that is not displayed to the user, such as the page title, meta tags, and links to external resources. The body element contains the main content of the page, including text, images, and other multimedia elements.

Let's take a closer look at each of the HTML page structure elements and their role in the page:

- *<!DOCTYPE html>*: The <!DOCTYPE html> element is the first element in an HTML page and tells the browser what version of HTML is being used. The latest version of HTML is HTML5, and the doctype for HTML5 is simply <!DOCTYPE html>.

- *<html>*: The <html> element is the root element of an HTML page and is used to define the entire structure of the page. It contains all the other elements of the page, including the head and body elements.

- *<head>*: The <head> element is used to provide information about the page that is not displayed to the user, such as the page title, meta tags, and links to external resources. The content within the head element is not visible to the user and is used by the browser to display the page correctly.

- *<title>*: The <title> element is used to define the title of the page, which is displayed in the browser's title bar and can also be used by search engines to display the page title in search results.

- *<meta>*: The <meta> element is used to provide additional information about the page, such as the page description, author, and keywords. These meta tags are used by search engines to help rank the page in search results.

- *<link>*: The <link> element is used to link to external resources, such as CSS stylesheets, JavaScript files, or other HTML pages.

- *<body>*: The <body> element contains the main content of the page, including text, images, and other multimedia elements. It is the visible part of the page that the user interacts with.

- *<header>*: The <header> element is used to define the header section of the page, which typically contains the site logo, navigation menu, and other header content.

- *<main>*: The <main> element is used to define the main content section of the page, which contains the primary content of the page.

- *<footer>*: The <footer> element is used to define the footer section of the page, which typically contains copyright information, contact information, and other footer content.

The HTML page structure is composed of several different elements, each with its own purpose and function. By understanding the basic structure of an HTML page and the role of each element, web developers can create well-structured and organized web pages that are easy to navigate and interact with. Additionally, adhering to best practices for HTML page structure can improve the page's search engine optimization (SEO) and overall user experience.

How CSS Works

Cascading Style Sheets is a technology used to define the look and feel of websites. CSS works by separating the presentation layer from the content layer of a web page, allowing designers to control the visual aspects of a site without affecting the underlying HTML code.

The basic principle of CSS is to apply styles to HTML elements. CSS styles are defined in a separate file or in a style block within the HTML file. Styles are written using a syntax that defines the type of element being styled, followed by the properties and values that define the appearance of the element.

For example, to define a style for a paragraph element, the following syntax might be used:

```
p {
    font-family: Arial;
    font-size: 22px;
    color: #bb0d10;
}
```

HTML Code:

```
<html>
    <body>
        <p>
            The properties font-family, font-size, and color
            are then defined, which set the font, font size,
            and color of the text within the paragraph element.
        </p>
        <link rel="stylesheet" href="../../css/example.css">
    </body>
</html>
```

15

Figure 1-6 shows what this code looks like in a browser.

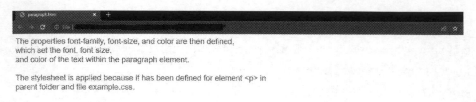

Figure 1-6. *CSS applied the font color for the <p> element*

In this example, the p selector targets all <p> elements in the HTML file. The properties font-family, font-size, and color are then defined, which set the font, font size, and color of the text within the paragraph element.

CSS works by flowing styles down from the parent element to its children. This means that if a style is defined for a parent element, it will be inherited by its child elements unless a different style is explicitly defined. For example, if a style is defined for the <body> element of a page, all elements within the body will inherit that style unless a different style is specified.

In addition to being cascading, CSS uses specificity to determine which styles should be applied to an element. Specificity refers to the weight or importance of a style rule. Styles with a higher specificity will override styles with a lower specificity. Specificity is determined by a combination of selectors, with more specific selectors taking precedence over less specific ones.

For example, a style rule that targets a specific ID will have a higher specificity than a rule that targets a class or element. The following example demonstrates this:

```
#header {
    background-color: blue;
}
```

```css
.header {
    background-color: red;
}
```

Here's the HTML code:

```html
<html>
    <body>
        <h1 id="header" class="header">This text is
        Heading 1.</h1>
        <link rel="stylesheet" href="../../css/example.css">
    </body>
</html>
```

As shown in Figure 1-7, the style rule that targets the #header ID will be applied, even though the .header class rule comes later in the file.

Figure 1-7. *Heading text with background color modified by CSS*

CSS also provides a range of layout and positioning options that allow designers to control the placement and arrangement of elements on a page. These include the float property, which allows elements to be positioned next to each other, and the position property, which allows elements to be positioned absolutely or relatively within their parent element.

In addition to these basic concepts, CSS provides a wide range of advanced features and techniques, such as media queries, animation, and responsive design. These features allow designers to create dynamic and interactive websites that adapt to a variety of screen sizes and devices. We are going to cover all these topics in later chapters.

CSS is a powerful technology that allows designers to control the appearance of web pages in a flexible and modular way. By separating the presentation layer from the content layer, CSS enables designers to create sophisticated and engaging websites that are easy to maintain and update. With its powerful layout and positioning options and advanced features, CSS is a critical tool for modern web design.

The Problem CSS Solves

CSS is a critical technology for modern web design. By separating the presentation layer from the content layer, CSS allows designers to create consistent, flexible, and accessible websites that are easy to maintain and update. With its wide range of styling options and advanced features, CSS is an essential tool for creating engaging and effective websites.

Web development is a complex process that involves many different technologies and tools. One of the most important technologies for web development is CSS, which is a stylesheet language that is used to define the visual appearance of web pages. CSS solves several common problems that web developers face when creating websites.

- *Consistency across pages*: One of the biggest challenges in web development is maintaining consistency across multiple pages. With CSS, developers can create a set of styles that can be applied to all pages on a website, ensuring a consistent look and feel. This makes it easier for users to navigate the website and helps to establish a strong brand identity.

- *Responsive design*: Another common problem in web development is creating websites that are optimized for different screen sizes and devices. CSS provides a range of tools and techniques for creating responsive designs, including media queries, flexible layouts, and viewport units. With these tools, developers can create websites that look great on desktops, laptops, tablets, and smartphones, without having to create separate designs for each device.

- *Browser compatibility*: One of the most challenging aspects of web development is ensuring that websites look and function correctly across different web browsers. CSS provides a standardized way of defining styles, which helps to ensure that websites look consistent across different browsers. Additionally, CSS provides fallback options for older browsers so that websites can still be viewed by users who may not have the latest software.

- *Separation of content and presentation*: One of the key principles of web development is the separation of content and presentation. CSS allows developers to create a clear separation between the content of a website and its visual appearance. This separation makes it easier to update the design of a website without affecting the underlying content and makes it easier to maintain and update the website over time.

- *Accessibility*: Accessibility is an important consideration in web development, as websites should be designed to be accessible to all users, including those with disabilities. CSS provides a range of tools and techniques for improving the accessibility of websites, such as using high-contrast colors, providing text alternatives for images, and using semantic HTML markup.

CSS is an essential technology for web development, as it solves many of the common problems that developers face when creating websites. CSS provides tools and techniques for maintaining consistency across pages, creating responsive designs, ensuring browser compatibility, separating content and presentation, and improving accessibility. With CSS, developers can create engaging and effective websites that are optimized for a wide range of users and devices.

CSS Selectors

CSS selectors are a powerful feature of Cascading Style Sheets that allow developers to target specific elements on a web page and apply styles to them. CSS selectors make it possible to create unique and complex styles for different elements and are an essential tool for creating effective and engaging web designs. In this section, we will explore the basics of CSS selectors and how they work.

CSS selectors are used to target specific elements on a web page, such as headings, paragraphs, links, and images. Selectors can be used to apply styles to individual elements or to groups of elements. There are several types of CSS selectors; each has its own syntax and functionality.

- *Type selectors*: Type selectors target elements based on their HTML tag name. For example, the selector h1 would target all heading level 1 elements on the page. Type selectors are the simplest type of selector and are often used to apply global styles to all elements of a particular type.

- *Class selectors*: Class selectors target elements based on their class attribute. The class attribute is used to assign a name to an element, which can then be targeted with a selector. For example, the selector .my-class would target all elements that have the class my-class assigned to them. Class selectors are often used to apply styles to specific groups of elements, such as navigation menus or buttons.

- *ID selectors*: ID selectors target elements based on their ID attribute. The ID attribute is used to assign a unique identifier to an element, which can then be targeted with a selector. For example, the selector #my-id would target the element that has the ID my-id assigned to it. ID selectors are often used to apply styles to specific elements, such as headers or footer sections.

- *Attribute selectors*: Attribute selectors target elements based on their attributes, such as the src attribute for images or the href attribute for links. Attribute selectors can be used to target elements based on specific attribute values or to target elements that have a particular attribute assigned to them.

- *Pseudo-classes and pseudo-elements*: Pseudo-classes and pseudo-elements are used to target elements based on their state or position within the document. Pseudo-classes are used to target elements based on user interactions, such as hovering over a link or clicking a button. Pseudo-elements are used to target specific parts of an element, such as the first letter of a paragraph or the content of a link.

CSS selectors are an essential tool for web developers, as they allow for precise targeting of specific elements on a web page. By using a combination of type selectors, class selectors, ID selectors, attribute selectors, pseudo-classes, and pseudo-elements, developers can create unique and complex styles for different elements on a web page. Understanding CSS selectors is a fundamental aspect of web development and is essential for creating effective and engaging web designs. All these selectors will be covered as part of later chapters.

Summary

This chapter covered the technologies used in web development. It also covered how HTML is rendered by a browser and its DOM tree, the different HTML elements, and the way it is being displayed by the browser using pseudo-code. It covered HTML page structure and how it can be defined in multiple ways. We also looked at how CSS works along with HTML and what kinds of problems can be solved using CSS and different CSS selectors.

CHAPTER 2

HTML5 and Responsive Web Design

This chapter covers HTML5 and responsive web design by describing the features that are supported by modern-day browsers. It covers how to create an HTML5 page and explains why it is easier to write pages with HTML5 than its older versions. The chapter also covers semantic elements and shows the code to make it easier to understand the practical usage. Additionally, the chapter explains text-level semantics in detail, followed by the audio and video capabilities. All these concepts are supported by code examples and browser screenshots displaying how a modern-day browser renders the code.

What HTML5 Features Are Supported by Browsers?

Most parts of HTML5 can be used today, as it is a widely supported standard across all modern browsers. However, some of the newer features may not be fully supported in older browsers, so before implementing

© Varun Gor 2023
V. Gor, *Creating Responsive Websites Using HTML5 and CSS3*,
https://doi.org/10.1007/978-1-4842-9783-4_2

a new feature, you should always check the browser version your app is going to run on. Here are some of the commonly used HTML5 features that are widely supported across all modern browsers:

- *Semantics*: HTML5 introduced a new set of semantic tags that can be used to describe the structure of web pages more accurately. These tags are designed to replace the generic <div> and <span> tags that were used in earlier versions of HTML. Some of the most popular semantic tags in HTML5 include <header>, <footer>, <nav>, <article>, and <section>. Search engine optimization can be improvised if these tags are utilized appropriately, since a search engine will use the new tags to understand the content of the web page.

- *Audio and video*: HTML5 provides built-in support for audio and video playback, which eliminates the need for third-party plugins like Adobe Flash. This makes it much easier to include multimedia content on web pages. The audio and video tags in HTML5 support several file formats, including MP3, MP4, and Ogg. They also include controls for playback, volume, and other settings, making it easy for users to interact with multimedia content.

- *Canvas*: The <canvas> element in HTML5 provides a way to draw graphics on a web page using JavaScript. This feature can be used to create dynamic visual effects, such as animations, games, and data visualizations. The <canvas> element can be used to create 2D or 3D graphics, and it provides a powerful set of APIs for manipulating the graphics.

- *Forms*: HTML5 includes several enhancements to forms, including new input types and attributes. Some of the new input types in HTML5 include email, URL, and number, which provide more accurate validation for user input. HTML5 also includes new form attributes, such as autocomplete and required, which improve the usability of forms.

- *Geolocation*: HTML5 provides a geolocation API that allows web applications to access the user's location. This feature can be used to create location-based services, such as maps, local search, and weather updates. The geolocation API is available on the latest web browsers, such as Chrome, Firefox, and Safari.

- *Local storage*: HTML5 provides a local storage API that permits web applications to use a user's computer to store data. This feature can be used to create web applications that work offline or to cache the data to load the web application faster. The local storage API works on the latest web browsers, such as Chrome, Firefox, and Safari.

- *Web workers*: HTML5 provides a web workers API that allows web applications to run scripts in the background. This feature can be used to improve the performance of web applications by offloading tasks to separate threads. The web workers API works on the latest web browsers, such as Chrome, Firefox, and Safari.

- *Web sockets*: HTML5 provides a web sockets API that allows web applications to create real-time, two-way communication channels between the client and the server. This feature can be used to create web applications that update in real time, such as chat applications, collaborative editors, and online gaming apps. The web sockets API works on the latest web browsers, such as Chrome, Firefox, and Safari.

How to Write HTML5 Pages

The way HTML page used to be written was something like the following code:

```
<!DOCTYPE html PUBLIC "-//W3C//DTD XHTML 1.0 Transitional//EN"
"http://www.w3.org/TR/xhtml1/DTD/xhtml1-transitional.dtd">
<html xmlns="http://www.w3.org/1999/xhtml">
<head>
<meta http-equiv="Content-Type" content="text/html;
charset=UTF-8" />
```

The HTML5 equivalent code, shown here, is the same as the previous code:

```
<!DOCTYPE html>
<html lang="en">
<head>
<meta charset=UTF-8 />
```

Save the previous code with an .html extension, and you have written your first HTML5 page according to the W3C validator (http://validator.w3.org)!

The first line of the code declares the new HTML5 doctype; remember, <!DOCTYPE html> and <!doctype html> are the same; the case does not make any difference.

The second tag is the first <html> tag, which mentions the language.

```
<html lang="en">
```

The <head> tag follows, with character encoding specified using <meta> (this is a void element and will not require a closing tag). The value for the character encoding will be UTF-8 (almost every time you create a HTML page) unless there is a specific requirement otherwise.

Writing HTML5 Code Is Easy

Developers have traditionally written code in HTML in lowercase and by surrounding multiple attributes with double quotes. But HTML5 lets you write code without quotes, in lower or uppercase, and with camel-case letters, and it doesn't need much information provided as an attribute in HTML tags.

Typically, CSS code in HTML would have href, rel, and type attributed, like so:

```
<link href="CSS/main.css" rel="stylesheet" type="text/css"/>
```

HTML5 does not require so many details; it will just work fine with the following declaration:

```
<link href=CSS/main.css rel=stylesheet >
```

If you look closely, there is no ending tag or closing slash, there are no quotes surrounding attribute values, and there is no type declaration either. Here both the examples are valid and would work just fine.

In addition to CSS and JavaScript elements, this kind of lenient syntax is applicable for all HTML tags. A <div> element could be defined as follows:

```
<div id=wrapper>
```

Let's take an example of another tag, for example, an <img> tag.

```
<img SRC=company_logo.png Alt=logo >
```

This HTML code is a valid <img> tag without an end tag or a slash, without quotes, and with mixing upper and lowercase. HTML even lets developers write code without specifying <html>, <body>, and <head> tags, and it still validates.

Although HTML5 is flexible, I still recommend writing a few extra lines of code to maintain best practices for better code maintainability and ease of understanding. Hence, writing code in the old style is beneficial. The CSS declaration shown earlier, for example, can be written as follows:

```
<link href="CSS/main.css" rel="stylesheet" />
```

The quotes and closing slash are in the stylesheet declaration, but the type attribute is omitted here. This HTML code would not be flagged.

The anchor tag has been revised and can do a few things that the prior version of HTML didn't support. The older HTML version needed each element to have its own anchor tag.

For example, look at the following code snippet:

```
<div class="container"><a href="home.html"> Home </a></div>
<p><a href="home.html"> This paragraph is actually a link
tagged by anchor. </a></p>
<h1><a href="home.html"> Navigate to Home Page </a></h1>
```

HTML5 now allows us to group all the elements under the anchor tag, and it doesn't require each element to have its own anchor tag. See the following code snippet:

```
<a>
    <div class="container"> Home </div>
    <p> This paragraph is actually a link tagged by
    anchor. </p>
    <h1> Navigate to Home Page   </h1>
</a>
```

The only restriction here with the anchor tag is that it cannot be grouped with another anchor tag, and form elements are not allowed to be grouped within the anchor tag.

There are some features of HTML5 that are obsolete; it won't complain if you use them, but you should avoid using them if you can. The HTML5 validator will generate warnings for these elements.

There are two types of obsolete features: conforming and nonconforming. The prior definition was for the conforming obsolete feature, whereas a nonconforming obsolete feature doesn't guarantee that it will work on all the browsers. It may work on a few but not others, so you should implement those types at your own risk. Here is where you can find a list of nonconforming obsolete features: `https://html.spec.whatwg.org/#non-conforming-features`.

Semantic Elements in HTML5

What are semantic elements? A semantic element defines its purpose or what type of content it will contain. A few examples of such semantic elements are <header>, <footer>, and <p> tags. HTML was invented as a markup language to provide a description of the documents it hosts, and it has evolved as the Internet has grown.

Initially the Internet was used to share scientific research material, and eventually people wanted to share other things on the Internet, followed up by people making their website look good. Building such functionality on the Web was not supported at that time, which forced developers to use work-arounds to make their websites look good. Nonsemantic elements did this job for the programmers (e.g., <div>) and provided these tags with class or id attributes, which in turn defined the purpose of the tag (e.g., <div class="header"></div>).

There are many advantages to using semantic elements. The first and foremost is that they make it easier to read code. They draw anyone's attention when they look at the code (either written by you or by someone else).

The following piece of code will illustrate my point; it uses semantic elements:

```
<header></header>
<section>
    <article>
        <figure>
            <img>
            <figcaption></figcaption>
        </figure>
    </article>
</section>
<footer></footer>
```

The following code uses nonsemantic elements:

```
<div id="header"></div>
<div class="section">
    <div class="article">
        <div class="figure">
            <img>
            <div class="figcaption"></div>
        </div>
    </div>
</div>
<div id="footer"></div>
```

Apart from better readability, semantic elements have greater accessibility. They are not restricted to readability; they can also be used as search engine optimization (SEO) and assistive technologies, which help users who have vision impairment. Overall, it's a better experience for all the users.

New Semantic Elements

Here are the new semantic elements:

- *<article>*: This element specifies an independent content. Use cases of article tags could be comments, news articles, blogs, etc.

    Here is what it looks like in code:

```
<style>
    .superheros {
      margin: 0;
      padding: 5px;
      background-color: lightgray;
    }

    .superheros > h1, .superhero {
      margin: 10px;
      padding: 5px;
    }

    .superhero {
      background: white;
    }
```

```
      .superheros > h2, p {
        margin: 4px;
        font-size: 90%;
      }
  </style>
  <article class="superheros">
      <h1>Most Liked Superheros</h1>
      <article class="superhero">
          <h2> Batman </h2>
          <p>Batman is a superhero appearing in American
          comic books published by DC Comics. <br/>
          The character was created by artist Bob Kane
          and writer Bill Finger, and debuted in the 27th
          issue of the comic book</p>
      </article>
      <article class="superhero">
          <h2> Iron Man</h2>
          <p>Iron Man is a superhero appearing in
          American comic books published by Marvel
          Comics. <br/>
          The character was co-created by writer and editor
          Stan Lee, developed by scripter Larry Lieber,
          and designed by artists Don Heck and Jack
          Kirby</p>
      </article>
  </article>
```

Figure 2-2 shows what it looks like in a browser (the paragraph in the code is taken from Wikipedia).

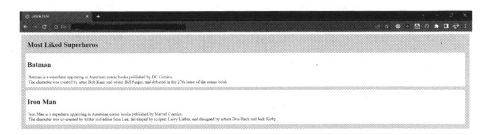

Figure 2-1. *Google Chrome displaying the new semantic tags*

- *<aside>*: As an addendum to the main content, <aside> is used to define a kind of subcontent or sidebar content.

Here is what it looks like in code:

```
<style>
    aside {
      width: 30%;
      padding-left: 15px;
      margin-left: 15px;
      float: right;
      font-style: italic;
      background-color: lightgray;
    }
</style>

<p>
    Marvel Comics is an American comic book publisher
    and the flagship property of Marvel Entertainment,
    a division of The Walt Disney Company since
    September 1, 2009. Evolving from Timely Comics
    in 1939,
```

```
        Magazine Management/Atlas Comics in 1951 and its
        predecessor, Marvel Mystery Comics, the Marvel
        Comics title/name/brand
        was first used in June 1961.

        Marvel was started in 1939 by Martin Goodman as
        Timely Comics,[3] and by 1951 had generally become
        known as Atlas Comics.
        The Marvel era began in June 1961 with the launch
        of The Fantastic Four and other superhero titles
        created by Stan Lee, Jack Kirby,
        Steve Ditko and many others. The Marvel brand,
        which had been used over the years and decades, was
        solidified as the company's
        primary brand.
    </p>
    <aside>
        <h3>
            Wolverine
        </h3>
        <p>
            The Wolverine, is a fictional character
            originating as the primary protagonist of 20th
            Century Fox's X-Men film series, <br/>
            and appearing in the Marvel Cinematic Universe
            media franchise produced by Marvel Studios.
        </p>
    </aside>
```

Figure 2-3 shows what it looks like in a browser (the paragraph in the code is taken from Wikipedia).

Marvel Comics is an American comic book publisher and the flagship property of Marvel Entertainment, a division of The Walt Disney Company since September 1, 2009. Evolving from Timely Comics in 1939, Magazine Management/Atlas Comics in 1951 and its predecessor, Marvel Mystery Comics, the Marvel Comics title/name/brand was first used in June 1961. Marvel was started in 1939 by Martin Goodman as Timely Comics,[3] and by 1951 had generally become known as Atlas Comics. The Marvel era began in June 1961 with the launch of The Fantastic Four and other superhero titles created by Stan Lee, Jack Kirby, Steve Ditko and many others. The Marvel brand, which had been used over the years and decades, was solidified as the company's primary brand.

> **Wolverine**
>
> *The Wolverine is a fictional character originating as the primary protagonist of 20th Century Fox's X-Men film series, and appearing in the Marvel Cinematic Universe media franchise produced by Marvel Studios.*

Figure 2-2. *Google Chrome displaying <aside> tag*

- *<details>*: This element is used to provide additional information that can be opened or closed based on user action. It can be assumed to be a pop-up or a widget that can be opened or closed.

Here is what it looks like in code:

```
<style>
    details > summary {
      padding: 4px;
      width: 200px;
      background-color: #5296ce;
      border: none;
      box-shadow: 1px 1px 2px #bbbbbb;
      cursor: pointer;
    }

    details > p {
      background-color: #5296ce;
      padding: 4px;
      margin: 0;
```

```
        box-shadow: 1px 1px 2px #bbbbbb;
    }
</style>

<details>
    <summary>
        ICC World Cup
    </summary>
    <p>
        The Cricket World Cup, officially known
        as ICC Men's Cricket World Cup,[4] is the
        international championship of
        One Day International (ODI) cricket. The event
        is organised by the sport's governing body, the
        International Cricket Council
        (ICC), every four years, with preliminary
        qualification rounds leading up to a finals
        tournament. The tournament is one of the
        world's most viewed sporting events and
        is considered the "flagship event of the
        international cricket calendar" by the ICC.[5]

        The first World Cup was organised in England
        in June 1975, with the first ODI cricket match
        having been played only four years
        earlier. However, a separate Women's Cricket
        World Cup had been held two years before the
        first men's tournament, and a
        tournament involving multiple international
        teams had been held as early as 1912, when a
        triangular tournament of Test matches
```

```
was played between Australia, England and South
Africa. The first three World Cups were held in
England. From the 1987
tournament onwards, hosting has been shared
between countries under an unofficial rotation
system, with fourteen ICC members
having hosted at least one match in the
tournament.
    </p>
</details>
```

Figure 2-3 shows what it looks like in a browser (the paragraph in the code is taken from Wikipedia). Figure 2-4 shows the HTML <details> tag expanded.

Figure 2-3. *HTML <details> tag collapsed*

Figure 2-4. *HTML <details> tag expanded*

- *<figcaption>*: Whenever a <figure> element needs a caption, the <figcaption> tag comes to rescue. This element can be placed as the first or last child of the <figure> element.

Here is what it looks like in code:

```
<style>
    figure {
      border: 1px #cccccc solid;
      padding: 4px;
      margin: auto;
    }

    figcaption {
      background-color: black;
      color: white;
      font-style: italic;
      padding: 2px;
      text-align: center;
    }
</style>
<figure>
    <img src="../../../cityscape.jpeg" alt="cityscape"
    style="width: 100%; height: 90%;" />
    <figcaption>High rise buildings in the city at
    night look so amazing.</figcaption>
</figure>
```

Figure 2-5 shows what it looks like in a browser.

Figure 2-5. *HTML <figcaption> tag displayed in Chrome*

- *<footer>*: There can be multiple elements in the footer section, and typically the footer element contains authorship, copyright, contact information, and a link to go to the top of the document.

Here is the code:

```
<style>
    footer {
        text-align: center;
        padding: 3px;
        background-color: DarkSalmon;
        color: white;
    }
</style>
<footer>
    <p>Author: John Doe<br>
        <a href="mailto:johndoe@example.com">
        johndoe@example.com</a>
    </p>
</footer>
```

Figure 2-6 shows what it looks like in a browser.

Figure 2-6. *HTML <footer> tag displayed in Chrome*

Note   The footer is placed after the figcaption tag and shows the author information.

- *<header>*: This element represents the introductory content for the document. Typically it contains navigation links, heading elements, or company logos.

  Here is the code:

  ```
  <style>
  header {
    display: block;
  }
  </style>
  ```

```
<header>
    <h1>Main page heading here</h1>
    <p>Posted by John Doe</p>
</header>
<style>
    figure {
      border: 1px #cccccc solid;
      padding: 4px;
      margin: auto;
    }

    figcaption {
      background-color: black;
      color: white;
      font-style: italic;
      padding: 2px;
      text-align: center;
    }
</style>
<figure>
    <img src="../../../cityscape.jpeg" alt="cityscape"
    style="width: 100%; height: 90%;" />
    <figcaption>High rise buildings in the city at
    night look so amazing.</figcaption>
</figure>
```

Figure 2-7 shows what it looks like in a browser.

Figure 2-7. *HTML <header> tag displayed in Chrome*

Note   The image tag is followed by the header tag.

- *<hgroup>*: This element can be used when the requirement is to have a heading with one or more subheadings. It is used to group heading elements from <h1> to <h6>.

Here is the code:

```
<hgroup>
    <h1>Heading H_One</h1>
    <h2>Heading H_Two</h2>
  <hgroup>
    <p>This is a sample text in paragraph 1.</p>
    <p>This is a sample text in paragraph 2.</p>
    <p>This is a sample text in paragraph 3.</p>
    <p>This is a sample text in paragraph 4.</p>
  </body>
```

Figure 2-8 shows what it looks like in a browser.

Figure 2-8. *HTML <hgroup> tag displayed in Chrome*

- *<main>*: As the name specifies, this tag is used to define the nonrepetitive content of the document. This tag should contain information unique to document; no content such as navigations, sidebars, or links should be repeated. Multiple definitions for the main tag per the documentation is not allowed, and it cannot be a descendent of <article>,<aside>, <header>, <footer>, or <nav> elements.

Here is the code:

```
<style>
    main {
      margin: 0;
      padding: 5px;
      background-color: rgb(91, 153, 161);
    }

    main > h1, p, .cricketer {
      margin: 10px;
      padding: 5px;
    }
```

43

```
    .cricketer {
      background: rgb(137, 116, 116);
    }

    .cricketer > h2, p {
      margin: 4px;
      font-size: 90%;
    }
</style>
<main>
    <h1>Most Popular Cricketers</h1>
    <p>The list of cricketer popular around the world
    is hard to fit in here.</p>
    <article class="cricketer">
      <h2>Sachin Tendulkar</h2>
      <p>Sachin Ramesh Tendulkar, AO is an Indian
      former international cricketer who captained the
      Indian national team.
        He is regarded as one of the greatest batsmen
        in the history of cricket. He is the all-time
        highest run-scorer in both ODI and
        Test cricket with more than 18,000 runs and
        15,000 runs, respectively.</p>
    </article>
    <article class="cricketer">
      <h2>Adam Gilchrist</h2>
      <p>Adam Craig Gilchrist AM is an Australian
      cricket commentator and former international
      cricketer and captain of the
        Australia national cricket team. He was an
        attacking left-handed batsman and record-
        breaking wicket-keeper, who redefined
```

```
      the role for the Australia national team
      through his aggressive batting.</p>
   </article>
   <article class="cricketer">
     <h2>Allan Donald</h2>
     <p>Allan Anthony Donald is a South African former
     cricketer who is also the current bowling coach
     of Bangladesh national cricket
        team. Often nicknamed 'White Lightning' due to
        his lightning quick bowling, he is considered
        one of the South Africa national
        cricket team's most successful pace
        bowlers.</p>
   </article>
 </main>
```

Figure 2-9 shows what it looks like in a browser (the paragraph in the code is taken from Wikipedia).

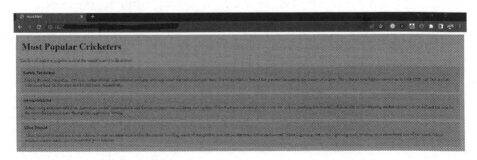

Figure 2-9. *HTML <main> tag displayed in Chrome*

- *<mark>*: This tag defines the text that should be highlighted.

Here is the code:

```
<style>
    mark {
        background-color: yellow;
        color: black;
    }
</style>
<p>Send <mark>bug report</mark>, holiday plan and
<mark>MOM</mark> to the higher management.</p>
```

Figure 2-10 shows what it looks like in a browser.

Send bug report, holiday plan and MOM to the higher management.

Figure 2-10. *HTML <mark> tag displayed in Chrome*

- *<nav>*: As the name suggests, the web application's navigation can be defined using this tag. Though it is not mandatory to define all the links inside the <nav> tag, it defines the majority of navigational links.

  Here is the code:

```
<nav>
    <a href="/html/">HTML</a> |
    <a href="/css/">CSS</a> |
    <a href="/js/">JavaScript</a> |
    <a href="/python/">Python</a>
</nav>
```

Figure 2-11 shows what it looks like in a browser.

HTML | CSS | JavaScript | Python

Figure 2-11. *HTML <nav> tag displayed in Chrome*

- *<section>*: The <section> element is used when a generic section of document needs to be defined.

Here is the code:

```
<style>
    section {
        display: block;
    }
</style>
<section>
    <h2>WWF History</h2>
    <p>The World Wide Fund for Nature (WWF) is an
    international organization working on issues
    regarding the conservation, research and
    restoration of the environment, formerly named the
    World Wildlife Fund. WWF was founded in 1961.</p>
</section>

<section>
<h2>WWF's Symbol</h2>
<p>The Panda has become the symbol of WWF. The
well-known panda logo of WWF originated from a
panda named Chi Chi that was transferred from the
Beijing Zoo to the London Zoo in the same year of
the establishment of WWF.</p>
</section>
```

Figure 2-12 shows what it looks like in a browser (the paragraph in the code is taken from Wikipedia).

WWF History

The World Wide Fund for Nature (WWF) is an international organization working on issues regarding the conservation, research and restoration of the environment, formerly named the World Wildlife Fund. WWF was founded in 1961.

WWF's Symbol

The Panda has become the symbol of WWF. The well-known panda logo of WWF originated from a panda named Chi Chi that was transferred from the Beijing Zoo to the London Zoo in the same year of the establishment of WWF.

Figure 2-12. *HTML <section> tag displayed in Chrome*

- *<address>*: The <address> element defines numerous ways of getting touch with the author or owner of the document. This tag can contain contact information such as email address, website link, postal address, phone number, or social media links. The information rendered in the <address> tag is in italic, and a line break is added before and after the <address> element by the majority of the browsers.

  Here is the code:

  ```
  <style>
      address {
          display: block;
          font-style: italic;
      }
  </style>
  <p>
      The properties font-family, font-size, and color
      are then defined, <br/>
      which set the font, font size, <br/>
      and color of the text within the paragraph element.
  ```

```
<br/><br/>
The stylesheet is applied because it has been
defined for element &lt;p&gt; in <br/>
parent folder and file example.css.
</p>
<link rel="stylesheet" href="../../css/example.css">
<address>
    Written by <a href="mailto:johndoe@example.com">Jon
    Doe</a>.<br>
    Visit us at:<br>
    Example.com<br>
    Box 564, Disneyland<br>
    USA
</address>
```

Figure 2-13 shows what it looks like in a browser (the paragraph in the code is taken from Wikipedia)..

Figure 2-13. *HTML <address> tag displayed in chrome*

- *<summary>*: This tag defines the heading for the <details> tag. The first child of the <details> tag must be a <summary> tag, which contains the information in a section that can be expanded or collapsed by a click of a button.

Here is what it looks like in code:

```
<style>
    details > summary {
      padding: 4px;
      width: 200px;
      background-color: #d9b37c;
      border: none;
      box-shadow: 1px 1px 2px #131313;
      cursor: pointer;
    }

    details > p {
      background-color: #d9b37c;
      padding: 4px;
      margin: 0;
      box-shadow: 1px 1px 2px #131313;
    }
</style>
<details>
    <summary>Marvel Comics</summary>
    <p>
        Marvel Comics is an American comic book
        publisher and the flagship property of Marvel
        Entertainment,
        a division of The Walt Disney Company since
        September 1, 2009. Evolving from Timely Comics
        in 1939,
        Magazine Management/Atlas Comics in 1951 and
        its predecessor, Marvel Mystery Comics, the
        Marvel Comics title/name/brand
        was first used in June 1961.
```

```
        Marvel was started in 1939 by Martin Goodman
        as Timely Comics,[3] and by 1951 had generally
        become known as Atlas Comics.
        The Marvel era began in June 1961 with the
        launch of The Fantastic Four and other
        superhero titles created by Stan Lee,
        Jack Kirby,
        Steve Ditko and many others. The Marvel brand,
        which had been used over the years and decades,
        was solidified as the company's
        primary brand.
      </p>
    </details>
```

Figure 2-14 shows how Google Chrome displays it (collapsed).

Figure 2-14. *HTML <summary> tag displayed in Chrome (collapsed)*

Figure 2-15 shows how Google Chrome displays it (expanded).

Figure 2-15. *HTML <summary> tag displayed in Chrome (expanded)*

- *<time>*: This tag defines the time or datetime.

  Here is what it looks like in code:

  ```
  <p>The office is open from <time>09:00</time> to
  <time>18:00</time> Monday to Friday.</p>
  ```

  ```
  <p>I have an appointment with the CEO on
  <time datetime="2023-02-28 20:00">last day of
  February</time>.</p>
  ```

Figure 2-16 shows what it looks like in a browser.

The office is open from 09:00 to 18:00 Monday to Friday.

I have an appointment with the CEO on last day of February.

Figure 2-16. *HTML <time> tag displayed in Chrome*

Text-Level Semantics in HTML5

Text-level semantics refer to the HTML elements that define the meaning of the text within a web page. These elements provide additional context and information about the content of a page, making it easier for search engines, screen readers, and other tools to understand and interpret the content. In HTML5, there are several new text-level semantic elements, including the following:*<mark>*: This element is used to highlight text that is relevant or important to the content on the page. This element can be used to highlight specific words or phrases or to indicate the location of a particular point within the text. A code example was given earlier in this book.

- *<time>*: This element is used to define a specific date or time within the document. Time-related information such as the publication date of an article, the time of an event, or any other date can be represented by the <time> element. A code example was given earlier in this book.

- *<abbr>*: This element is used to define an abbreviation or acronym within the document. Additional context information and information about the meaning of a particular word or phrase can be emphasized by this element.

Here is what it looks like in code:

```
<style>
    abbr {
        display: inline;
    }
</style>
<p><dfn><abbr title="Cascading Style Sheets">CSS</abbr>
</dfn> is a language that describes the style of an
HTML document.</p>
```

Figure 2-17 shows what it looks like in a browser.

Figure 2-17. *HTML <abbr> tag displayed in Chrome*

- *<q>*: A short quotation within a document is written inside the <q> element. The primary focus of this element is to provide additional context and information about a particular quote or to indicate the author of a quote.

Here is what it looks like in code:

```
<style>
    q {
       color: gray;
       font-style: italic;
    }
</style>
<p>WWF's goal is to:
    <q>Build a future where people live in harmony with
    nature.</q>
    We hope they succeed.
</p>
```

Figure 2-18 shows what it looks like in a browser.

Figure 2-18. *HTML <a> tag displayed in Chrome*

- *<cite>*: This element is used to define a citation within the document. The primary focus of <cite> is to provide additional context and information about the source of a particular piece of information.

Here is what it looks like in code:

```
<style>
    cite {
        font-style: italic;
        color: rgb(126, 126, 237);
    }
</style>
<p><cite>The sport of cricket</cite> has a known
history beginning in the late 16th century. Having
originated in south-
east England,
    it became an established sport in the country in
    the 18th century and developed globally in the 19th
    and 20th centuries.
    International matches have been played since the
    19th-century and formal Test cricket matches are
    considered to date from 1877.</p>
```

Figure 2-19 shows what it looks like in a browser (the paragraph in the code is taken from Wikipedia).

Figure 2-19. *HTML <cite> tag displayed in Chrome*

Why Are Text-Level Semantics Important?

Text-level semantics are important because they help to improve the accessibility and usability of web content. By providing additional context and information about the content of a page, these elements make it easier for people with disabilities to understand and navigate the content.

For example, the <mark> element can be used to indicate the location of a particular point within the text. This can be particularly useful for people with visual impairments, who may find it difficult to navigate through large blocks of text.

Similarly, the <abbr> element can be used to provide additional context and information about the meaning of a particular word or phrase. This can be particularly useful for people with cognitive disabilities, who may have difficulty understanding certain words or concepts.

In addition to improving accessibility, text-level semantics can also improve the search engine optimization of a web page. By providing additional context and information about the content of a page, these elements make it easier for search engines to understand and index the content, which can lead to better search engine rankings and increased traffic to the site.

How to Use Text-Level Semantics

Using text-level semantics is relatively simple. All you need to do is identify the elements that are most appropriate for the content on your page and use them accordingly.

For example, if you are required to add a quote on your page, the <q> element can be used to define the quote, and the <cite> element can be used to define the source of the quote. Similarly, if you have an abbreviation or acronym on your page, you could use the <abbr> element to define the meaning of the word or phrase.

Audio and Video Capabilities of HTML5

The introduction of the <video> and <audio> tags in HTML5 has made the plug-ins that were used to embed the video and audio file on the website useless. A video file can be featured on the web page using the <video> element.

Let's take a look at a code example:

```
<!DOCTYPE html>
<html>
    <body>
        <video width="1080" height="720" controls>
            <source src="../../../sample.mp4" type=video/mp4>
        </video>
    </body>
</html>
```

Figure 2-20 shows what it looks like in a browser.

Figure 2-20. *HTML <video> tag displayed in Chrome*

The <video> element must define the following attributes in order work correctly:

- *src*: The URL where the video content is hosted.

- *type*: The video file format that will be used to play the content.

- *controls*: To control the playback content, this attribute is a must; without this attribute, the end user will not be able to play, pause, or seek the video content.

Additionally, the following are option controls that help influence the video content:

- *autoplay*: This starts the video as soon as it loads on the web page.

- *loop*: As the name specifies, the video content will be repeated once it is finished playing.

- *poster*: This defines an image or thumbnail for the video, and it is displayed when the content is not played.

- *preload*: When the page loads, how the video content is loaded can be specified by this attribute.

HTML5 supports three types of video files, as listed in Table 2-1.

Table 2-1. *Video Formats Supported by the HTML5 <video> Tag*

Format	MIME Type
mp4	video/mp4
webm	video/webm
ogg	video/ogg

Another way of inserting videos from an external source could be done by using iframes. Follow these steps to get the YouTube URL link:

1. Open the video on YouTube.

2. Right-click the video and click "<> copy embed code."

3. Paste the copied code onto a Notepad src tag, and will have the YouTube video source link; you will be using it for your src attribute of the video tag.

The following is some sample code:

```
<!DOCTYPE html>
<html>
  <body>
    <h2>Steve Jobs - How to Live before You Die</h2>
    <p>At his Stanford University commencement speech, Steve
    Jobs, CEO and co-founder of Apple and Pixar, urges us to
    pursue our dreams and see the opportunities in life's
    setbacks - including death itself.</p>
    <iframe width="500" height="320" src="https://www.youtube.
    com/embed/lcZDWo6hiuI">
    </iframe>
  </body>
</html>
```

The <audio> tag can be used to embed an audio file in the web page. Just like the <video> tag, the <audio> tag has the controls and source attributes that identify the file and whether to show the controls on the web page.

Here is what it looks like in code:

```
<h3>Ambient Classic Guitar</h3>
<audio controls autoplay>
    <source src="../../../sample_audio.mp3" type="audio/mpeg">
</audio>
```

Figure 2-21 shows what it looks like in a browser.

Figure 2-21. *HTML <audio> tag displayed in Chrome*

The HTML DOM controls the audio by defining properties, methods, and events that help to load, play, and pause audios, as well as set the duration and volume. The HTML DOM events can be used to notify when an audio begins to play, is paused, etc.

HTML5 supports the audio formats shown in Table 2-2.

Table 2-2. *Audio Formats Supported by the HTML5 <audio> Tag*

Format	MIME Type
mp3	audio/mpeg
wav	audio/wav
ogg	audio/ogg

Summary

This chapter covered the features of HTML5 that can be used to create a responsive web design. It explained the new features supported by this technology and listed the features such as the semantics, audio, and video capabilities added to HTML, as well as the canvas, geolocation, local storage, web works, and web sockets. We also explained how to write a new HTML5 web page, ways to make the job easier, and new features added to HTML5.

CHAPTER 3

Cascading Style Sheets and Layouts

This chapter covers CSS and layouts. This chapter will explain how to create and use floats in CSS3, as well as explaining the issues faced when working with floats and how to resolve them. Next, the chapter will cover box-sizing versus border-box, which one to use, and how to resolve issues if there are any during implementing them. Then, the chapter will explain how to implement a flexbox layout using CSS3, by providing HTML and CSS code and showing how the browser renders this code. It will explain various attributes and their values as well as how to arrange flex items and what properties they can have. The CSS grid layout is the next topic, covering details such as aligning and spacing grid items and sizing each item in the layout.

CSS and Responsive Design

Cascading Style Sheets (CSS) is an essential tool for web developers to create visually appealing websites. With the release of CSS3, developers have gained access to a plethora of new features that make designing websites much easier and more efficient. One of the most significant improvements in CSS3 is the ability to create complex and dynamic layouts

© Varun Gor 2023
V. Gor, *Creating Responsive Websites Using HTML5 and CSS3*,
https://doi.org/10.1007/978-1-4842-9783-4_3

without the need for external libraries or frameworks. In this chapter, we will explore three ways to build layouts using CSS3.

- **Flexbox**

  A flexbox is a powerful model that enables developers to design responsive and dynamic layouts quickly. A flexbox works by defining a container and its child elements, which are referred to as *flex items*. With a flexbox, you can easily align and distribute items within a container, adjust their sizes, and reorder them without affecting the HTML structure. The display property of the parent element is set to flex, and the layout properties for the child elements are defined to create a flex container. The most commonly used properties in a flexbox are justify-content, align-items, and flex-wrap.

- **Grid**

  A CSS grid is another powerful layout model that enables developers to create complex layouts with ease. With a CSS grid, you can define a grid container, divide it into rows and columns, and then place elements anywhere within that grid. A grid offers much more control over positioning than a flexbox and is particularly useful for creating multicolumn layouts. To use a grid, you need to define a grid container and specify its properties, such as grid-template-columns, grid-template-rows, and grid-gap. Once the grid container is defined, the grid-column and grid-row attributes can be used to place the items inside the grid.

- **Floats**

  Floats are a legacy technique for creating layouts still widely used today. Floats work by "floating" an element to one side of its container, allowing other content to flow around it. This technique is useful for creating multicolumn layouts and wrapping text around images. To use floats, you need to set the float attribute of an element to either left or right and then specify the width and margin properties to control its positioning. While floats can be useful for simple layouts, they have limitations and are not recommended for complex designs.

CSS3 offers developers a range of powerful tools for creating dynamic and responsive layouts. Flexbox and grid are the most commonly used layout models and offer a lot of flexibility and control over positioning. Floats are still useful for simple layouts but should be avoided for complex designs. By mastering these three techniques, developers can create visually appealing and responsive websites that work across multiple devices and platforms.

Using Floats

The CSS3 float property allows you to position an element to the left or right of its containing parent block, allowing other elements to flow around it. What float does is take out the element from its normal document flow and position it in relation to its parent element.

Here is some example code:

```
<!DOCTYPE html>
<html>
<head>
    <style>
        /* The container div */
        .container {
            width: 600px;
            margin: 0 auto;
            background-color: cornsilk;
            padding: 10px;
        }

        /* The left floated div */
        .left {
            float: left;
            width: 200px;
            background-color: crimson;
            padding: 10px;
            margin-right: 20px;
        }

        /* The right floated div */
        .right {
            float: right;
            width: 200px;
            background-color: darkolivegreen;
            padding: 10px;
            margin-left: 20px;
        }
    </style>
</head>
```

```
<body>
    <div class="container">
        <div class="left">
            <p>This is a left floated div.</p>
            <p>Other elements will flow around it.</p>
        </div>
        <div class="right">
            <p>This is a right floated div.</p>
            <p>Other elements will flow around it.</p>
        </div>
        <p>This is some text that will flow around the floated
        divs.</p>
    </div>
</body>
</html>
```

This code example has a parent container <div> with two child <div>s; the first one is floated to the left, and the second one is floated to the right. We also have a paragraph element after the floated <div>s that flows around them.

The .left and .right classes specify the float property, as well as the width, background color, padding, and margin properties. The .container class specifies the width, margin, background color, and padding properties.

Note that when using floats, it is important to clear them afterward to prevent unexpected layout behavior. This can be done by using the clear property or by using a clearfix hack.

Figure 3-1 shows how the code is displayed in a browser.

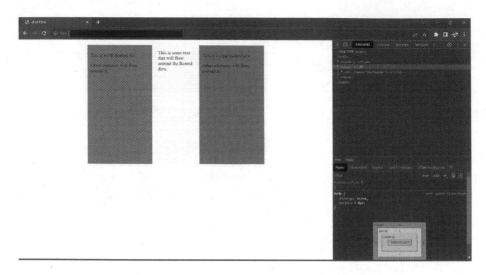

Figure 3-1. *Chrome browser displaying how float is used*

When working with CSS floats, it's common to encounter issues where floated elements do not behave as expected, such as when the containing element doesn't expand to contain its floated children or when subsequent elements are unintentionally affected by the float.

CSS clearfix will come to rescue to fix this problem, which is a technique to force a container element to expand and contain its floated children. Let's look at an example of how to use a clearfix.

Here is some code without the clearfix:

```
<!DOCTYPE html>
<html>
<head>
    <style>
        /* The container div with clearfix */
        /*.container:after {
            content: "";
            display: table;
            clear: both;
        }*/
```

```
        /* The left floated div */
        .left {
            float: left;
            width: 200px;
            background-color: cornflowerblue;
            padding: 10px;
            margin-right: 20px;
        }

        /* The right floated div */
        .right {
            float: right;
            width: 200px;
            background-color: sienna;
            padding: 10px;
            margin-left: 20px;
        }
    </style>
</head>
<body>
    <div class="container">
        <div class="left">
            <p>This is a left floated div.</p>
            <p>Other elements will flow around it.</p>
        </div>
        <div class="right">
            <p>This is a right floated div.</p>
            <p>Other elements will flow around it.</p>
        </div>
```

```
        <p>This is some text that will flow around the floated
        divs.</p>
    </div>
</body>
</html>
```

Figure 3-2 shows how the code is displayed in a browser.

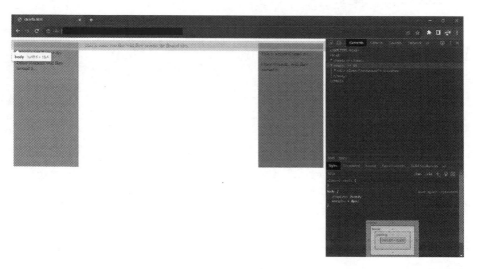

Figure 3-2. *Chrome browser displaying how a float is used without clearfix*

Here is some code with clearfix:

```
<!DOCTYPE html>
<html>
<head>
    <style>
        /* The container div with clearfix */
        .container:after {
            content: "";
            display: table;
```

```
        clear: both;
    }

    /* The left floated div */
    .left {
        float: left;
        width: 200px;
        background-color: cornflowerblue;
        padding: 10px;
        margin-right: 20px;
    }

    /* The right floated div */
    .right {
        float: right;
        width: 200px;
        background-color: sienna;
        padding: 10px;
        margin-left: 20px;
    }
    </style>
</head>
<body>
    <div class="container">
        <div class="left">
            <p>This is a left floated div.</p>
            <p>Other elements will flow around it.</p>
        </div>
        <div class="right">
            <p>This is a right floated div.</p>
            <p>Other elements will flow around it.</p>
        </div>
```

```
        <p>This is some text that will flow around the floated
        divs.</p>
    </div>
</body>
</html>
```

Figure 3-3 shows how the code is displayed in a browser.

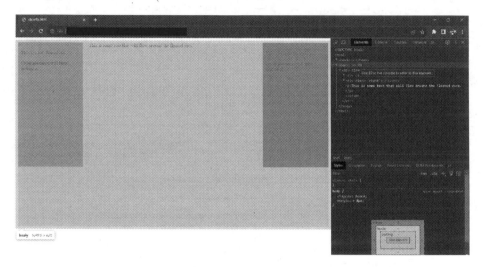

Figure 3-3.   *Chrome browser displaying how float is used with clearfix*

In this example, the .container class now has an :after pseudo-element with the content property value set to a blank string, display property set to table, and clear property set to both. This creates a pseudo-element after the container element and clears any floated elements within it, forcing the container to expand and contain its floated children.

Note that the clearfix technique can be applied to any container element with floated children and can also be achieved using other methods such as using the overflow property or using a separate element with the clear property.

Building a Float Layout

Consider the following HTML and CSS code. You can name the HTML file however you'd like, and the CSS should be named style.css (or you need to modify the link attribute to point to the correct CSS file).

Here's the HTML file:

```
<!DOCTYPE html>
<html>
<head>
    <title>Float Layout Example</title>
    <link rel="stylesheet" type="text/css" href="style.css">
</head>
<body>
    <header>
        <h1>My Website</h1>
    </header>

    <nav>
        <ul>
            <li><a href="#">Home</a></li>
            <li><a href="#">About</a></li>
            <li><a href="#">Contact</a></li>
        </ul>
    </nav>

    <main>
        <h2>Welcome to my website!</h2>
        <p>Lorem ipsum dolor sit amet, consectetur adipiscing
        elit. Sed in ante vitae arcu vulputate suscipit sit
        amet non massa. In hac habitasse platea dictumst. Sed
        tempor elit a urna vulputate hendrerit. Proin vitae
        massa non augue posuere bibendum. Nulla laoreet sodales
        leo, vel egestas lorem feugiat at.</p>
```

```
    </main>

    <footer>
        <p>&copy; 2023 My Website. All rights reserved.</p>
    </footer>
</body>
</html>
```

The text comes from https://loremipsum.io/.

Here is style.css:

```css
body {
    margin: 0;
    padding: 0;
    font-family: Arial, sans-serif;
}

header {
    background-color: #c73636;
    padding: 20px;
}

nav {
    float: left;
    width: 20%;
    background-color: aquamarine;
    height: 500px;
}

nav ul {
    list-style: none;
    padding: 0;
    margin: 0;
}
```

```
nav li {
    padding: 10px;
}

nav a {
    text-decoration: none;
    color: #333;
}

main {
    float: none;
    width: 100%;
    background-color: wheat;
    padding: 20px;
    height: 460px;
}

footer {
    clear: both;
    background-color: #ccc;
    padding: 20px;
    color: #fff;
    text-align: center;
}
```

In this example, the layout consists of a header, navigation bar, main content section, and footer. The navigation bar and main content section are positioned side by side using the float property. The footer element has a clear property that ensures it appears below the floated elements.

Figure 3-4 shows the Chrome browser displaying the float layout.

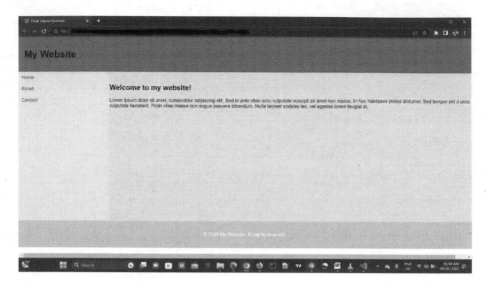

Figure 3-4. *Chrome browser displaying the float layout*

Box-Sizing or Border-Box

An element's box-model size can be controlled by the box-sizing property in CSS. By default, the size of an element is calculated based on its content, padding, border, and margin. However, with box-sizing, you can change this behavior to calculate the size of an element based on different box models.

There are two values for the box-sizing property: content-box and border-box.

- *content-box*: This is the box-sizing property's default value. When box-sizing: content-box is applied to an element, the element's dimensions are calculated based on its content, padding, and border. Any margin applied to the element is added to its total width and height.

- *border-box*: When box-sizing: border-box is applied to an element, the element's dimensions are calculated based on its content, padding, border, and margin. The total height and width of the element include its padding and border, but not any margin applied to it.

When content-box is used, the width is the addition of widths of content, margins, padding, and border as opposed to border-box, which is adjusting its width of content to accommodate the margins, padding, and border. Let's look at some examples.

The CSS for main and nav are modified, and a new definition of container is added.

When main or nav is modified with margin or padding with content-box, look athow the browser is displaying the content. Also note that the nav definition is using a box-sizing: content-box.

Here is the CSS code:

```css
body {
    margin: 0;
    padding: 0;
    font-family: Arial, sans-serif;
}

header {
    background-color: #c73636;
    padding: 20px;
}

nav {
    float: left;
    width: 200px;
    background-color: aquamarine;
```

```
    height: 500px;
    box-sizing: content-box;
}

nav ul {
    list-style: none;
    padding: 0;
    margin: 0;
}

nav li {
    padding: 10px;
}

nav a {
    text-decoration: none;
    color: #333;
}

main {
    float: none;
    width: 1000px;
    background-color: wheat;
    padding: 20px;
    height: 460px;
}

footer {
    clear: both;
    background-color: #ccc;
    padding: 20px;
    color: #fff;
    text-align: center;
}
```

```
container {
    width: 1200px;
}
```

Here is the HTML code:

```
<!DOCTYPE html>
<html>
<head>
    <title>Float Layout Example</title>
    <link rel="stylesheet" type="text/css" href="style.css">
</head>
<body class="container">
    <header>
        <h1>My Website</h1>
    </header>

    <nav>
        <ul>
            <li><a href="#">Home</a></li>
            <li><a href="#">About</a></li>
            <li><a href="#">Contact</a></li>
        </ul>
    </nav>

    <main>
        <h2>Welcome to my website!</h2>
        <p>Lorem ipsum dolor sit amet, consectetur adipiscing
        elit. Sed in ante vitae arcu vulputate suscipit sit
        amet non massa. In hac habitasse platea dictumst. Sed
        tempor elit a urna vulputate hendrerit. Proin vitae
        massa non augue posuere bibendum. Nulla laoreet sodales
        leo, vel egestas lorem feugiat at.</p>
    </main>
```

```
<footer>
    <p>&copy; 2023 My Website. All rights reserved.</p>
</footer>
</body>
</html>
```

Figure 3-5 shows how it looks in a browser (the paragraph comes from `https://loremipsum.io/`).

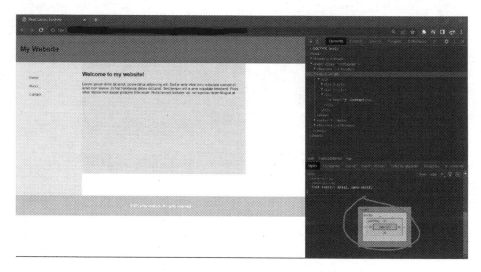

Figure 3-5. *Chrome browser displaying the float layout with content-box*

Observe that the nav width of 200px and padding of 100px is added to the box and the nav content is out of place.

Let's use border-box and check how Google Chrome displays it; here box-sizing: border-box in nav css definition is changed. See Figure 3-6.

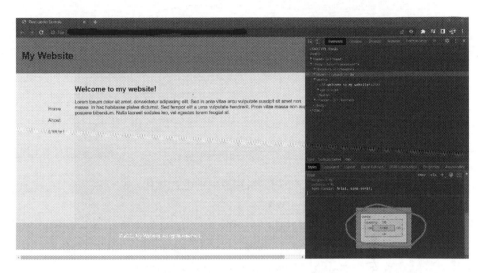

Figure 3-6. *Chrome browser displaying the float layout with border-box*

Introduction to Flexboxes

CSS3 has brought a lot of exciting new features to the field of web development, and one of the most powerful is the flexbox layout system. A flexbox, which means "flexible box layout," is a flexible and easy-to-use system for laying out elements in a container. It allows you to control the alignment, size, and distribution of elements with just a few simple properties, making it an essential tool for creating modern, responsive web designs.

One of the key benefits of a flexbox is its simplicity. With just a few lines of CSS, you can create complex and flexible layouts that would be difficult or impossible with traditional CSS layout techniques. To create a flexbox, a container element that encapsulates all the elements you want to lay out needs to be created. By changing the display property value to flex (display: flex), any HTML element can be turned into a flex container; let that HTML element be a <div> or a section.

79

Once you have your container set up, you can start using the various flexbox properties to control the layout of the elements inside it. Some of the most important properties include flex-direction, justify-content, align-items, and flex-wrap.

- *flex-direction* is used to determine two things: the main axis of the flex container and the direction in which the flex items are organized. It can be set to row, which is the default, to organize the items in a row from left to right. Alternatively, you can set it to row-reverse to lay out the items from right to left or column-reverse to lay them out in a column from top to bottom. column-reverse can also be used to lay out the items from bottom to top.

- *justify-content* controls how the items are aligned along the main axis of the flex container. It can be set to a number of different values, including flex-start, flex-end, center, space-between, space-around, and space-evenly. flex-start aligns the items to the start of the container, flex-end aligns them to the end, and center aligns them to the center. space-between is used when items need to be aligned with equal space in between them along the main axis, while space-around distributes the items with equal space on their left and right sides. Finally, space-evenly distributes the items with equal space between and around them.

- *align-items* controls how the flex items are organized along the cross-axis of the container, which is perpendicular to the main axis. By default the value is stretch, which stretches the items to fill the entire cross-axis. Alternatively, you can set it to flex-start to align them to the start of the cross-axis, flex-end to align them to the end, center to align them to the center, or baseline to align them to the baseline of the text.

- *flex-wrap* controls if the flex items should wrap to the next line or stay on the same line. The default value is set to nowrap, which means that the items will stay on the same line and may overflow the container. However, this value can be set to wrap that permits the items to wrap to the next line as needed. wrap-reverse can also be used to wrap the items to the next line in reverse order.

- Finally, *flex-grow*, *flex-shrink*, and *flex-basis* control the size and flexibility of the individual flex items. flex-grow determines the growth of an item in relation to other items in the container, flex-shrink determines the factory by which an item can shrink, and flex-basis is used to set the initial size of the flex items before any remaining space.

Flexbox Overview

CSS has revolutionized the way web pages are designed and structured. One of the most powerful CSS features is the flexbox, a layout model that lets developers create flexible and responsive designs with ease. Whether you're an experienced web developer or just a beginner, understanding the fundamentals of a flexbox is essential for building modern, dynamic web interfaces. In this section, we will provide an overview of a flexbox, exploring its core concepts and demonstrating how it can streamline your CSS layouts.

What is a flexbox? A flexbox, short for "flexible box layout," is a CSS layout model designed to provide a way to create a container that effectively arranges, distributes, and aligns the elements within it. With Flexbox, you can create responsive and dynamic layouts that adapt to different screen sizes and orientations.

- *The flex container and flex items*: To use a flexbox, a flex container and its children known as flex items must be defined. The value flex for the display attribute (display: flex) creates a flex container and enables flexbox properties for its child elements. This allows you to control the layout and positioning of the child elements known as flex items within the container.

- *Main axis and cross axis*: The flexbox layout introduces two main axes: the main axis and the cross axis. The primary axis along which the flex items are aligned is the main axis, while the cross axis runs vertically to it. The direction of the main axis can be defined using the flex-direction property, which can be set to row, row-reverse, column, or column-reverse. This flexibility enables both horizontal and vertical layouts.

- *Alignment and distribution*: Flexbox provides a powerful mechanism to arrange and spread flex items along the main axes as well as cross axes. Some of the key properties include the following:

  - *justify-content*: How flex items are aligned along the main axes is controlled by justify-content.

  - *align-items*: This aligns flex items along the cross axis.

- *align-content*: This provides an additional space along the cross axis when multiple rows or columns of flex items need to be accommodated in the container.

- *Flex item properties*: Flex items have properties that allow you to control their behavior within the flex container. Some commonly used properties include the following:

  - *flex-grow*: This specifies how flex items will spread to fill available space.

  - *flex-shrink*: This determines the ability of flex items to shrink when space is limited.

  - *flex-basis*: The initial size of a flex item is defined first, and the remaining space is distributed across the flex items within the container.

  - *order*: This controls the order in which flex items appear within the container.

- *Responsive layouts with Flexbox*: Flexbox excels at creating responsive layouts that adapt to different screen sizes and orientations. By combining flexible sizing options, media queries, and other CSS techniques, you can build dynamic interfaces that seamlessly adjust to varying devices and viewport dimensions.

- *Browser pupport and compatibility*: A flexbox is widely supported in modern browsers, including Chrome, Firefox, Safari, and Edge. However, for older versions of Internet Explorer, partial support is available using the -ms- prefix.

A flexbox is a powerful CSS layout model that enables developers with a versatile toolset to create flexible and responsive web designs. By understanding the core concepts of a flexbox and its various properties, you can streamline your CSS layouts and build modern interfaces that adapt seamlessly to different devices. With its widespread browser support, a flexbox is a valuable addition to any developer's toolkit. So, dive into the world of flexbox and take your web layouts to new heights!

Arranging the Flex Items

In CSS3, you can use a flexbox layout to align and space flex items within a flex container. A flexbox provides several properties that control the flex items' space and alignment within the container. Let's go through the main properties you can use:

- *Justify content*: The alignment of the flex items along the main axis of the container is controlled by the justify content property. It defines how the extra space is spread between and around flex items. The following are the possible values:

  - *flex-start*: Items are aligned at the start of the container.

  - *flex-end*: Items are aligned at the end of the container.

  - *center*: Items are centered within the container.

  - *space-between*: Items are evenly spread with space between them.

  - *space-around*: The space around the flex items is distributed evenly.

  - *space-evenly*: The flex items will be aligned by spacing them evenly in the container.

- *Align items*: The alignment of the flex items along the cross axis of the container is controlled by align items property. It determines how items are aligned within their respective lines. The possible values are as follows:

    - *flex-start*: Items are aligned at the start of the cross axis.

    - *flex-end*: Items are aligned at the end of the cross axis.

    - *center*: Items are centered along the cross axis.

    - *stretch*: Items are stretched to fill the container along the cross axis.

    - *baseline*: Flex items' baseline will determine their alignment.

- *Align self*: The only difference between align-items and align-self is that align-self allows flex items to be aligned individually within the container. It takes the same values as align-items.

- *Align content*: Multiple lines of flex items can be arranged along the cross axis by using this property, in case they wrap into multiple lines. The possible values are similar to justify-content but apply to the cross axis.

- *Flex item margins*: You can also use regular CSS margin properties to add space around individual flex items. An alternate to this is gap, which can be applied to flex container and will do the same job as margins.

- *Order*: All the flex elements are of order 0 and displayed in the same order as defined in the HTML. If you want to re-order the elements, the order property can be given a value to less than 0 to move the flex item ahead or greater than 0 to move the flex item after the flex item having the default order.

Here's the code for style.css:

```css
.container {
    font-family: sans-serif;
    background-color: bisque;
    font-size: 34px;

    /* Flexbox */
    display: flex;
    align-items: center;
    justify-content: flex-start;
    gap: 30px;

}

.element--1 {
    align-self: flex-start;
    background-color: yellowgreen;
}

.element--2 {
    background-color: burlywood;
}

.element--3 {
    background-color: turquoise;
    height: 150px;
}
```

```css
.element--4 {
    background-color: springgreen;
}

.element--5 {
    align-self: stretch;
    order: 1;
    background-color: slategray;
}
```

HTML file:-

```html
<!DOCTYPE html>
<html>
    <head>
        <title>Float Layout Example</title>
        <link rel="stylesheet" type="text/css"
        href="style.css">
    </head>
    <body>
        <div class="container">
            <div class="element--1">1</div>
            <div class="element--2">2</div>
            <div class="element--3">3</div>
            <div class="element--4">4</div>
            <div class="element--5">5</div>
        </div>
    </body>
</html>
```

Figure 3-7 shows how the code looks in a browser.

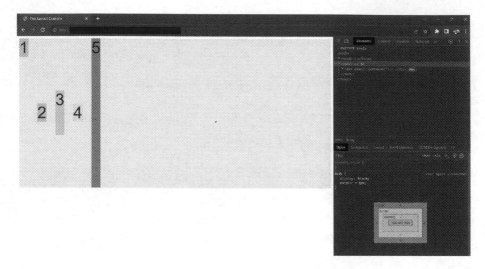

Figure 3-7. *Chrome browser displaying the flexbox layout*

Properties of Flex

In CSS, the flex property is a shorthand property that combines three individual properties: flex-grow, flex-shrink, and flex-basis. It is used to control the behavior and sizing of flex items within a flex container.

The flex property accepts up to three values.

- *flex-grow*: It is possible for one flex item to grow in comparison to other flex items within the same container. How much it will grow can be determined by the flex-grow property. It takes a non-negative number as a value. By default, all flex items have a flex-grow value of 0, which means they won't grow to fill the available space. If you set a positive value, such as flex: 1, the item will grow proportionally to other items with positive flex-grow values.

- *flex-shrink*: It is possible for one flex item to shrink in comparison to other flex items within the same container. How much it will shrink can be determined by the flex-shrink property. It takes a non-negative number as a value. By default, all flex items have a flex-shrink value of 1, which means they can shrink equally. If you set a value of 0, the item will not shrink. If you set a higher value, such as flex: 2, the item will shrink twice as much as other items with flex-shrink set to 1.

- *flex-basis*: The initial size of the flex items can be defined by this property after the remaining space is distributed. It can be specified as a length value (e.g., pixels, percentages) or the keyword auto. The default value is auto, which means the item's size is based on its content or the value of its width or height properties. You can also use flex-basis to explicitly set a specific size for the flex item.

Here are a few examples of how the flex property can be used:

```css
.flex-item {
    flex: 1; /* Equivalent to flex-grow: 1, flex-shrink: 1,
    flex-basis: 0 */
}

.flex-item {
    flex: 0 0 200px; /* No growth, no shrinking, initial width
    of 200 pixels */
}

.flex-item {
    flex: 2 1 auto; /* Twice the growth compared to other
    items, default shrinking, initial size based on content */
}
```

By utilizing the flex property, you have control over how flex items grow, shrink, and establish their initial size within a flex container.

Building a Flexbox Layout

Here is the code for flex.html:

```
<!DOCTYPE html>
<html>
    <head>
        <title>Float Layout Example</title>
        <link rel="stylesheet" type="text/css"
        href="style.css">
    </head>
    <body>
        <div class="container">
            <div class="el element--1">1</div>
            <div class="el element--2">2</div>
            <div class="el element--3">3</div>
            <div class="el element--4">4</div>
            <div class="el element--5">5</div>
        </div>
    </body>
</html>
```

Here is the code for style.css:

```
.container {
    font-family: sans-serif;
    background-color: bisque;
    font-size: 34px;
```

```css
    /* Flexbox */
    display: flex;
    align-items: center;
    justify-content: space-between;
    gap: 30px;
}

.el {
    flex: 1;
    padding: 10px;
    border: 1px solid #ccc;
}

.element--1 {
    align-self: flex-start;
    background-color: yellowgreen;
}

.element--2 {
    background-color: burlywood;
}

.element--3 {
    background-color: turquoise;
    height: 150px;
}

.element--4 {
    background-color: springgreen;
}
```

```
.element--5 {
    align-self: stretch;
    order: 1;
    background-color: slategray;
}
```

The flex container has three flex items in the previous code example. The display property converts the normal container into a flex container. The justify-content property is set to space-between, which places an equal space between the items. The align-items property is set to center, which vertically centers the items within the container.

The .item class has a flex property set to 1, which allows the items to grow and shrink equally to fill the available space. We also add some padding and styling to make the items visually distinguishable.

You can customize the layout by adjusting the flex properties and other CSS properties to meet your specific needs. Feel free to modify the code as desired.

Figure 3-8 shows how the code looks in a browser.

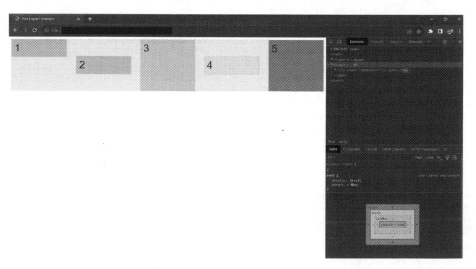

Figure 3-8. *Chrome browser displaying the flexbox layout with adjusting the flex item*

Introduction to CSS Grid

The CSS grid is a powerful layout system introduced in CSS3 that allows developers to create complex and responsive grid-based layouts on web pages. It provides a wide range of features and properties that enable precise control over placing and aligning flex items within a grid.

Before CSS grids, web developers relied on various techniques such as floats, positioning, and flexboxes to achieve grid-like layouts. While these techniques were useful, they often required complex CSS rules and were not specifically designed for creating grid layouts. CSS grid, on the other hand, was built from the ground up to address these limitations and provide a more intuitive and efficient way to create grid-based designs.

The main concept behind a CSS grid is the division of a web page into a series of rows and columns. Elements within these rows and columns can be placed and arranged according to the desired layout. The grid container serves as the parent element that holds the grid items, which are the individual elements being positioned within the grid.

To start using the CSS grid layout, you first define a grid container by applying the display: grid property to a parent element. This establishes the grid context for its child elements. Once the grid container is set, you can specify the size and behavior of the rows and columns using the grid-template-rows and grid-template-columns properties. These properties allow you to define fixed sizes, use flexible proportions, or even use keywords like auto to automatically adjust the size based on the content.

Elements within the grid container can be positioned using the grid-row and grid-column properties. These properties determine the starting and ending positions of an element within the grid, allowing you to create both simple and complex layouts. Additionally, the row and column positions can be defined by the grid-area property in a single declaration.

The CSS grid also offers powerful alignment and spacing options. You can align elements vertically or horizontally within their respective grid cells using properties such as justify-items, align-items, justify-content, and align-content. These properties enable precise control over the positioning of grid items. Furthermore, the grid-gap property allows you to define the spacing between rows and columns, providing flexibility in adjusting the overall grid layout.

One of the most powerful features of a CSS grid is its ability to handle responsive design seamlessly. By utilizing media queries and the grid-template-areas property, you can create different grid layouts for different screen sizes. This flexibility makes it easier to build responsive websites that adapt to various devices and screen resolutions.

The CSS grid is a game-changer for web layout design. With its intuitive syntax and powerful capabilities, it simplifies the creation of grid-based layouts, offers precise control over element positioning and alignment, and enables seamless responsiveness. Whether you are a beginner or an experienced developer, mastering the CSS grid layout opens up a world of possibilities for creating modern and visually appealing web designs. So, dive into CSS grid and elevate your web layout skills to the next level!

CSS Grid: Revolutionizing Web Layout Design

The CSS grid layout system has revolutionalized the way web developers create and manage website layouts. With its introduction in CSS3, the CSS grid provides a powerful and flexible solution for designing complex grid-based structures with ease. In this section, we will explore the fundamental concepts and features of CSS grid and understand how it has reshaped the landscape of web design.

What Is a CSS Grid?

A CSS grid is a two-dimensional layout model that allows developers to create grid-based designs by dividing a web page into rows and columns. Unlike previous layout methods such as floats and positioning, a CSS grid provides a dedicated system designed specifically for building grids, making it more intuitive and efficient.

Defining a Grid

To start using a CSS grid, we designate an element as the grid container by applying the display: grid property. This establishes the grid context for its child elements, turning them into grid items. Once the container is defined, we can set up the rows and columns by using properties such as grid-template-rows and grid-template-columns, specifying their sizes and proportions or using keywords like auto to dynamically adjust based on content.

Placing Grid Items

A CSS grid offers accurate control over the placement of grid items within the grid container. We can specify the starting and ending positions of an item within the grid using properties such as grid-row-start, grid-row-end, grid-column-start, and grid-column-end. These properties allow us to create both simple and complex layouts by precisely positioning items in the desired grid cells.

Grid Lines and Areas

Grid lines play a crucial role in a CSS grid as they define the boundaries of rows and columns. By utilizing line-based placement, we can position items not only within cells but also across multiple cells. Additionally, a

CSS grid introduces the concept of grid areas. With the grid-area property, we can assign names to areas within the grid and easily position items in those areas using the grid-area value.

Alignment and Spacing

A CSS grid provides powerful alignment and spacing options to control the positioning of grid items. Properties such as justify-items, align-items, justify-content, and align-content allow us to align items vertically and horizontally within their grid cells or adjust the overall alignment of items within the grid container. Moreover, the grid-gap property enables us to define the spacing between rows and columns, allowing for precise control over the layout's spacing and rhythm.

Responsive Design with CSS Grid

One of the standout features of a CSS grid is its ability to handle responsive design effortlessly. By combining media queries with different grid configurations, developers can create different layouts for different screen sizes. Using the grid-template-areas property, we can assign grid areas to specific sections of the layout and rearrange them dynamically as the screen size changes. This flexibility empowers us to build responsive websites that seamlessly adapt to various devices and screen resolutions.

Browser Support

A CSS grid enjoys widespread browser support, making it accessible to a vast majority of web users. All the latest browsers, including Google Chrome, Firefox, Safari, and Edge, have excellent support for CSS grids. Additionally, with the use of vendor prefixes, developers can ensure compatibility with older browser versions.

In conclusion, a CSS grid is a groundbreaking layout system that has revolutionized web design. Its intuitive syntax, extensive features, and excellent browser support make it a go-to choice for creating responsive, flexible, and visually appealing grid-based layouts. By mastering CSS grids, developers can unlock a new level of creativity and efficiency in web layout design, enabling them to build modern, dynamic websites that engage and delight users. So, embrace CSS grids and embark on an exciting journey to reshape the digital landscape.

Sizing Grid Columns and Rows

The CSS grid layout has revolutionized web design by providing a powerful and flexible way to create grid-based layouts. One of the key aspects of CSS grids is the ability to size grid columns and rows according to our design requirements. In this section, we will explore different methods and techniques for sizing grid columns and rows effectively.

- *Understanding the grid template*: Before manipulating sizing, it's important to grasp the concept of the grid template. The grid template defines the structure of the grid by specifying the number of rows and columns it should have. Here's an example:

```
.grid-container {
    display: grid;
    grid-template-columns: 1fr 2fr 1fr;
    grid-template-rows: auto 100px;
}
```

In this example, we have three columns with a flexible width ratio of 1:2:1 and two rows, one with an automatic height and the other with a fixed height of 100 pixels.

- *Using fixed sizes*: To set fixed sizes for grid columns and rows, we can use specific length units like pixels (px) or any other appropriate unit. For instance:

```
.grid-container {
    display: grid;
    grid-template-columns: 200px 300px;
    grid-template-rows: 100px 150px;
}
```

The previous code example will create a grid with two columns, the first being 200 pixels wide and the second 300 pixels wide. Similarly, the grid will have two rows, with the first being 100 pixels tall and the second 150 pixels tall.

- *Utilizing flexible sizes*: CSS grids also provide a powerful way to create flexible sizes for grid columns and rows. This approach allows the grid to adjust its layout dynamically based on available space. The fr unit is used to define these flexible sizes. Here's an example:

```
.grid-container {
    display: grid;
    grid-template-columns: 1fr 2fr;
    grid-template-rows: 1fr auto;
}
```

In this case, the first column occupies one-third of the grid's width, while the second column occupies two-thirds. The first row takes one-third of the grid's height, while the second row expands to fit its content.

- *Combining fixed and flexible sizes*: In many cases, a combination of fixed and flexible sizes is required to achieve the desired layout. CSS Grid allows us to mix these approaches within the grid template. For example:

```
.grid-container {
    display: grid;
    grid-template-columns: 1fr 200px 2fr;
    grid-template-rows: auto 100px;
}
```

Here, the first column and the third column have flexible sizes that adapt to the available space, while the middle column maintains a fixed width of 200 pixels. The first row adjusts its height based on content, and the second row has a fixed height of 100 pixels.

Sizing grid columns and rows in a CSS grid layout gives developers fine-grained control over their web layouts. By combining fixed and flexible sizes intelligently, we can create versatile and responsive grid-based designs. Understanding the grid template and utilizing length units like pixels and the fr unit empowers us to craft layouts that meet our design goals. Experiment with different sizing techniques to achieve visually appealing and adaptive grid layouts with a CSS grid.

Placing and Aligning Grid Items

To place and align grid items in a CSS grid layout, there are numerous properties and values you can use various properties and values. Here's an overview of the most commonly used ones:

- *grid-template-columns and grid-template-rows*: These properties define the size and number of columns and rows in your grid. You can specify the size using absolute units (pixels, percentages) or relative units (fr, auto).

  Here's an example:

  ```
  .grid-container {
      display: grid;
      grid-template-columns: 1fr 2fr 1fr;
      grid-template-rows: auto 100px;
  }
  ```

- *grid-column and grid-row*: These properties specify the starting and ending positions of an item within the grid by referring to the column and row lines.

  Here's an example:

  ```
  .grid-item {
      grid-column: 2 / 4; /* Starts at the 2nd column
      line and ends at the 4th column line */
      grid-row: 1; /* Starts at the 1st row line and ends
      at the 1st row line (same row) */
  }
  ```

- *grid-area*: A single declaration that can declare the item's size and position is achieved using the grid-area attribute by using the grid area's name.

  Here's an example:

  ```
  .grid-item {
      grid-area: header; /* Refers to a named grid area
      called "header" */
  }
  ```

- *justify-self and align-self*: The individual grid items can be aligned using this attribute within their cells along the horizontal (justify) and vertical (align) axes.

  Here's an example:

  ```
  .grid-item {
      justify-self: center; /* Centers the item
      horizontally within its cell */
      align-self: end; /* Aligns the item to the bottom
      of its cell */
  }
  ```

- *justify-items and align-items*: These properties set the default alignment for all grid items within the grid container.

  Here's an example:

  ```
  .grid-container {
      justify-items: center; /* Centers all items
      horizontally within their cells */
      align-items: stretch; /* Stretches all items
      vertically to fill their cells */
  }
  ```

These are just a few examples of how you can place and align grid items in a CSS grid layout. By combining these properties and values, you can create various grid layouts and achieve precise control over the positioning and alignment of your elements.

Building a CSS Grid Layout

CSS Grid is a powerful layout system that permits the creation of complex and flexible grid-based designs. Let's see an example of how you can create a basic grid layout.

Here is style.css:

```css
.grid-container {
    display: grid;
    grid-template-columns: 1fr 1fr 1fr; /* Three columns with
    equal width */
    grid-gap: 10px; /* Gap between grid items */
}

.item {
    background-color: #cd3434;
    padding: 20px;
}
```

Here is grid.html:

```html
<!DOCTYPE html>
<html>
    <head>
        <title>Float Layout Example</title>
        <link rel="stylesheet" type="text/css"
        href="style.css">
    </head>
    <body>
        <div class="grid-container">
            <div class="item">Item 1</div>
            <div class="item">Item 2</div>
            <div class="item">Item 3</div>
            <div class="item">Item 4</div>
```

```
    <div class="item">Item 5</div>
    <div class="item">Item 6</div>
  </div>
  </body>
</html>
```

In the previous example, we have a container with the class grid-container that displays as a grid. The grid-template-columns property defines the number and width of the grid columns. In this case, we have three columns, each with equal width (1fr).

The grid-gap property adds a gap of 10 pixels between grid items.

The item class is applied to each grid item. In this example, I've given them a background color and some padding to make them visually distinct.

Feel free to adjust the number of columns, gap size, and styling as per your requirements. You can also use different units such as pixels, percentages, or auto for column widths to create more complex grid layouts.

Figure 3-9 shows what it looks like in a browser.

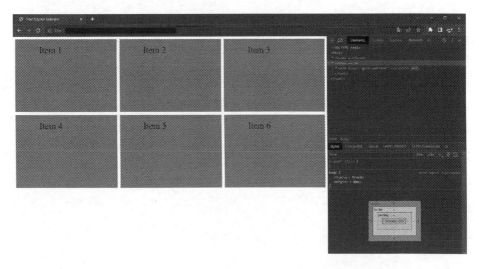

Figure 3-9. *Chrome browser displaying the CSS grid layout*

Summary

This chapter covered various topics related to CSS layouts and how to implement them. We covered how to create and use floats, box-sizing, and border-box. The chapter also covered flexboxes and how to create them along with its attributes and their explanation. We talked about the flex items in the flexbox layout and covered the properties of the flex. We showed how to implement a CSS grid layout along with sizing grid columns and rows and placing and aligning the grid items.

CHAPTER 4

Media Queries

In the era of smartphones, tablets, and multitudes of screen sizes, creating a seamless user experience across devices has become crucial. Responsive web design allows websites to adapt and respond to different viewport sizes, providing optimal viewing experiences. CSS3 introduced a powerful feature called *media queries* that enables developers to tailor stylesheets based on various device characteristics. In this chapter, we will explore what media queries are, how they work, and their significance in creating responsive designs.

What Are Media Queries?

Media queries are a CSS3 feature that allows developers to apply different stylesheets or specific styles within a stylesheet based on the characteristics of the device or viewport. These characteristics include viewport width, height, device type, orientation, resolution, and more. By utilizing media queries, developers can create designs that adapt gracefully to different devices and ensure the content remains readable and usable across various screen sizes.

© Varun Gor 2023
V. Gor, *Creating Responsive Websites Using HTML5 and CSS3*,
https://doi.org/10.1007/978-1-4842-9783-4_4

Media queries work by evaluating the media features specified within the query and applying the associated styles if the conditions are met. The general syntax of a media query consists of an @media rule followed by one or more media features enclosed within parentheses. Here's an example of a basic media query:

```
@media (max-width: 768px) {
    /* Styles to apply when viewport width is 768px or less */
}
```

In this example, the styles within the curly braces will be applied when the viewport width is 768 pixels or less. Media queries can also include logical operators such as *and*, *not*, and *only* to combine multiple media features for precise targeting.

Common Media Features

Here are the common media features:

- *Width and height*: The width and height media features allow developers to apply styles based on the viewport dimensions. For example:

```
@media (max-width: 600px) {
    /* Styles for viewport width 600px or less */
}

@media (min-height: 768px) {
    /* Styles for viewport height 768px or more */
}
```

- *Device type*: Media queries can also target specific device types, such as the screen, print, speech, and more. This allows for tailored styles for different output devices. For example:

```
@media screen {
    /* Styles for screen devices */
}

@media print {
    /* Styles for print media */
}
```

- *Orientation*: The orientation media feature enables developers to differentiate between portrait and landscape orientations of the device. For example:

```
@media (orientation: landscape) {
    /* Styles for landscape orientation */
}

@media (orientation: portrait) {
    /* Styles for portrait orientation */
}
```

- *Resolution*: Media queries can target devices based on their display resolution, ensuring high-resolution assets are used when necessary. For example:

```
@media (min-resolution: 300dpi) {
    /* Styles for devices with high-resolution
    displays */
}
```

Significance of Media Queries

Media queries are integral to creating responsive web designs that adapt to the ever-expanding range of devices and screen sizes. They allow developers to craft interfaces that provide a consistent user experience, regardless of whether the user is on a desktop, smartphone, or tablet. By utilizing media queries effectively, websites can improve readability, usability, and overall user satisfaction.

Media queries in CSS3 empower developers to build responsive web designs that gracefully adapt to various devices and screen sizes. By targeting specific media features, such as width, height, orientation, and resolution, developers can apply custom styles to ensure a seamless user experience. With the continued growth of mobile and diverse screen sizes, understanding and implementing media queries is essential for creating modern, user-friendly websites that cater to a wide range of devices and user preferences.

How Does a Media Query Work?

This section covers how to define a media query. Consider the following CSS code.

Here is `style.css`:

```css
.container {
    background-color: cadetblue;
    width: 1920px;
    height: 1080px;
    clear: both;
}
```

```css
@media screen and (max-width : 920px) {
    .container {
        background-color: crimson;
        clear: both;
    }
}

@media screen and (max-width : 780px) {
    .container {
        background-color: plum;
        clear: both;
    }
}

@media screen and (max-width : 600px) {
    .container {
        background-color: darkgreen;
        clear: both;
    }
}

@media screen and (max-width : 360px) {
    .container {
        background-color: seagreen;
        clear: both;
    }
}
```

Here is the HTML file:

```
<!DOCTYPE html>
<html>
    <head>
        <title>Media Query Example</title>
        <link rel="stylesheet" type="text/css"
        href="style.css">
    </head>
    <body>
        <div class="container"></div>
    </body>
</html>
```

How does Google Chrome display this with different resolution sizes? See Figure 4-1 through Figure 4-4. (Note: As the browser size is changing, the background color for <div> will change as defined in the CSS.)

Figure 4-1. *Media query code displayed full screen (1080px)*

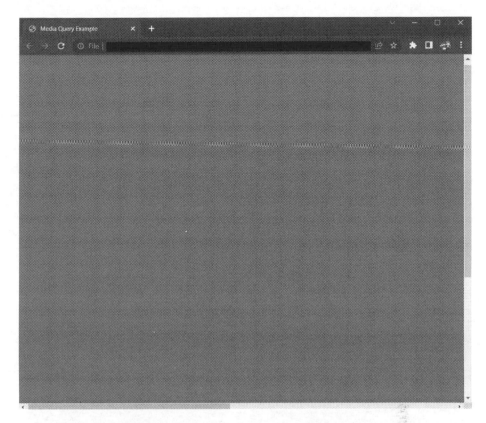

Figure 4-2. *Media query code displayed at 920px*

Figure 4-3. *Media query code displayed at 780px*

Figure 4-4. *Media query code displayed at 600px*

The media query focuses on styling the web page based on the device's capabilities; in other words, if the device is able to load the styles, they will be applied.

With this example, we have seen just one condition, max-width, but media queries can work with a variety of other conditions. Loading a device-specific (or conditional) CSS file is also possible, as shown here:

```
@import url("tab.css") screen and (max-width : 480px);
```

Note that, when used, this will be added to the HTTP request and may affect the loading time of your web page.

When building media queries, most often the size and resolution of the device are of primary focus, targeting the device's viewport (the visible part of the website for one particular device). However, media queries can be tested with various parameters. As mentioned earlier, they can be tested on width and height and device-width and device-height. In addition, the aspect-ratio and color parameters can be tested. Most of the options can be tested in a range by using the min and max options.

Building a Simple Media Query Project

Here is the CSS code:

```
.container{
    display: flex;
    flex-direction: column;
    height: 100vh;

   /* Creating gap between rows  */
    gap: 30px;
  }
```

```
[class ^="row-"]{
  display: flex;
  flex-direction: row;

 /* Creating gap between boxes */
  gap : 30px;
}

[class ^="box-"]{

  background-color: #eae672;
  font-size: 90px;
  padding: 10px;
  border: 2px solid black;
  box-sizing: content-box;

 /* Place letter at the center */
  display: grid;
  place-items: center;
}

@media screen and (max-width: 650px){

  /* Change orientation */
    [class ^="row-"]{
      flex-direction: column;
    }

  /* Change width of boxes */
    [class ^="box-"]{
      width: 100%;
    }
  }
```

Here is the HTML code:

```html
<html>
    <head>
        <title>Media Query Example</title>
        <link rel="stylesheet" type="text/css" href="mq.css">
    </head>
    <body>
        <div class="container">

            <div class="row-1">
                <div class="box-1"><img src="../../../../../
                images/ace-gc9bd94751_1280.png" width="100px"
                height="100px"></div>
                <div class="box-2"><img src="../../../../../
                images/clubs-g847a850ff_1280.png" width="100px"
                height="100px"></div>
                <div class="box-3"><img src="../../../../../
                images/five-g98e284f73_1280.png" width="100px"
                height="100px"></div>
            </div>

            <div class="row-2">
                <div class="box-4"><img src="../../../../../
                images/nine-g12e3b987e_1280.png" width="100px"
                height="100px"></div>
                <div class="box-5"><img src="../../../../../
                images/playing-card-g1c01e2707_1280.png"
                width="100px" height="100px"></div>
                <div class="box-6"><img src="../../../../../
                images/playing-card-g721103018_1280.png"
                width="100px" height="100px"></div>
            </div>
```

```
    <div class="row-3">
        <div class="box-7"><img src="../../../../../
        images/playing-card-g81e13fa7e_1280.png"
        width="100px" height="100px"></div>
        <div class="box-8"><img src="../../../../../
        images/playing-card-gda6f55dd7_1280.png"
        width="100px" height="100px"></div>
        <div class="box-9"><img src="../../../../../
        images/spades-gf13173e2d_1280.png"
        width="100px" height="100px"></div>
    </div>
    </div>
    </body>
</html>
```

Note   The references for images in the code need be changed as per the availability.

Figure 4-5 and Figure 4-6 show how it looks in a browser.

Figure 4-5. *Media query code displayed in desktop version*

117

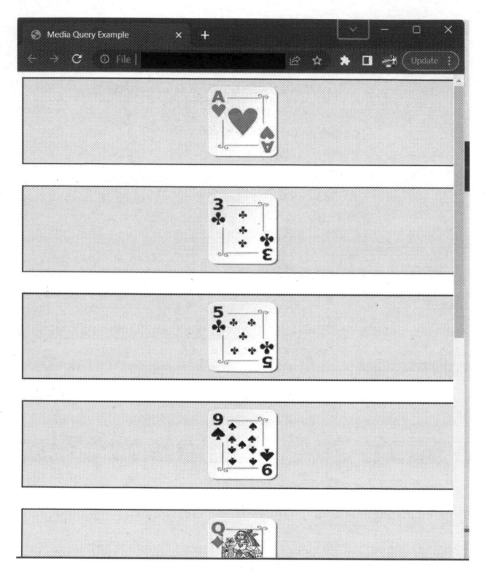

Figure 4-6. *Media query code displayed in mobile version*

Summary

This chapter talked about media queries and how to use them. We started with what a media query is, followed by how a media query works., we built a simple media query project to better understand how they work.

CHAPTER 5

CSS Selectors, Color Modes, and More

CSS3 is a powerful tool. In this chapter, we discuss CSS selectors, color modes, custom modes such as font-face, and custom typography. This chapter explains the building blocks of styling, vendor prefixes, and multiple column layout. The chapter will talk about the issues of styles and how to resolve them and well as cover the new CSS selectors and how to implement them. It will cover how strings can be manipulated using CSS3. Then we will discuss custom web typography and @font-face topics, as well as CSS3 color formats and the different ways in which they can be used. Of course, we'll give code examples and show browser screenshots.

Exploring the Power of CSS3

In the ever-evolving world of web development, front-end developers play a crucial role in creating engaging and visually stunning user interfaces. Cascading Style Sheets has been the backbone of web design for decades, and with the introduction of CSS3, front-end developers have gained access to a whole new set of powerful tools and features. CSS3 has revolutionized the way websites and applications are designed, enabling developers to create stunning visual effects, responsive layouts, and

© Varun Gor 2023
V. Gor, *Creating Responsive Websites Using HTML5 and CSS3*,
https://doi.org/10.1007/978-1-4842-9783-4_5

dynamic user experiences. In this chapter, we will delve into the exciting capabilities that CSS3 offers to front-end developers and how it has transformed the web development landscape.

- *Enhanced styling and visual effects*: CSS3 introduces an array of new styling features that allow developers to push the boundaries of design. With CSS3, you can easily apply gradients, shadows, rounded corners, and transformations to elements, giving them a modern and polished appearance. Animations and transitions can be created using CSS3, enabling developers to bring life to static web elements and captivate users with smooth and eye-catching effects. The ability to manipulate colors, text, borders, and backgrounds with greater control gives developers the freedom to create unique and visually appealing interfaces.

- *Responsive web design*: One of the most significant contributions of CSS3 to front-end development is its support for responsive web design. Responsive design ensures that websites and applications adapt seamlessly to different screen sizes and devices, providing an optimal viewing experience for users. CSS3 introduces media queries, which enable developers to define specific styles for different screen sizes and orientations. This flexibility allows websites to automatically adjust their layout, font sizes, and image sizes based on the user's device, eliminating the need for separate mobile versions. By leveraging CSS3's responsive design capabilities, front-end developers can ensure that their creations are accessible and visually appealing across a wide range of devices.

- *Flexbox and grid layouts*: CSS3 introduces two powerful layout modules: flexbox and CSS grid. A flexbox provides a flexible and efficient way to create dynamic and responsive layouts. It simplifies the process of aligning, spacing, and distributing elements within a container, making it ideal for building navigation menus, card-based designs, and complex user interfaces. A CSS grid, on the other hand, offers a two-dimensional grid system, allowing developers to create complex and grid-based layouts with ease. It enables precise control over the placement and sizing of elements within the grid, offering endless possibilities for creating advanced website layouts. Both flexbox and CSS grid layouts have revolutionized front-end development by providing intuitive and efficient methods for building responsive and complex designs.

- *Custom fonts and typography*: CSS3 brings a new level of control over typography and font usage. With the @font-face rule, front-end developers can embed custom fonts into web pages, giving them the freedom to choose from a vast array of typefaces. This feature eliminates the need to rely on system fonts, allowing developers to create unique and consistent typography experiences. CSS3 also offers greater control over letter spacing, line height, and text decoration, enabling developers to fine-tune the visual appearance of text. These typography enhancements have significantly improved the aesthetics and readability of web content.

- *Better browser compatibility*: CSS3 has played a vital role in driving browser innovation and standardization. Although not all CSS3 features are fully supported in older browsers, most modern browsers have excellent compatibility with CSS3 specifications. Developers can use progressive enhancement techniques and fallback options to ensure graceful degradation in older browsers while taking full advantage of CSS3 features in modern ones. With the increasing adoption of evergreen browsers, front-end developers can confidently leverage the power of CSS3 to enhance their designs without worrying about compatibility issues.

Understanding the Building Blocks of Styling

At the core of CSS lies CSS rules, which define how specific elements should be styled. In this section, we will dissect the anatomy of a CSS rule and explore its key components, helping you understand the building blocks of styling in CSS.

- *Selector*: The selector is the first part of a CSS rule and determines which HTML elements the rule applies to. Selectors can target elements based on their tag names, class names, IDs, attributes, or even position within the document structure. For example, the selector .container targets all elements with the class container, while the selector #header targets an element with the ID of header. Selectors are crucial as they define the scope of the styling rule.

- *Property*: The property is the second part of a CSS rule and specifies the aspect of the element that will be styled. Properties can control various aspects such as color, size, font, spacing, positioning, and more. Common properties include color, font-size, margin, background-image, and border-radius. The choice of properties depends on the desired visual effect or behavior you want to achieve.

- *Value*: The value is the third part of a CSS rule and assigns a specific setting or measurement to the property. The value determines how the property will be applied to the selected elements. For example, for the property color, values can be specific color names (red, blue, green), hexadecimal color codes (#FF0000, #00FF00, #0000FF), or RGB values (rgb(255, 0, 0)). The available values depend on the property being used.

- *Declaration*: The combination of the property and its corresponding value forms a declaration. Declarations are enclosed within curly braces, {}, and are placed inside a CSS rule. Multiple declarations can exist within a single CSS rule, each separated by a semicolon. For example:

```
h1 { color: red; font-size: 24px; }
```

In this example, color: red; and font-size: 24px; are two declarations within the CSS rule targeting h1 elements.

- *Rule set*: A rule set is a collection of one or more CSS declarations enclosed within curly braces. It consists of a selector and one or more declarations associated with that selector. Multiple rule sets can exist within a CSS stylesheet, allowing developers to apply different styles to different elements or groups of elements.

- *CSS rule cascade*: CSS rules can have multiple declarations targeting the same element or group of elements. In such cases, the CSS rule cascade comes into play. The cascade determines which declaration takes precedence based on factors such as specificity, inheritance, and order of appearance in the stylesheet. Understanding the cascade is crucial for resolving conflicts and ensuring the desired styles are applied correctly.

In summary, mastering the anatomy of a CSS rule is essential for front-end developers as it forms the foundation of styling web pages. By understanding selectors, properties, values, declarations, and the cascade, developers gain the power to control the visual aspects of HTML elements. With this knowledge, you can confidently craft stunning designs, create responsive layouts, and bring your creative vision to life on the Web.

The Power of Vendor Prefixes

When it comes to developing websites and applications, ensuring cross-browser compatibility is crucial. Different browsers often interpret CSS properties and features differently, leading to inconsistencies in the visual presentation. Vendor prefixes, also known as *browser prefixes*, are an essential tool that allows front-end developers to target specific browser implementations and ensure the consistent rendering of CSS styles. In this section, we will explore what vendor prefixes are, why they are necessary, and how to effectively use them in CSS.

- *Understanding vendor prefixes*: Vendor prefixes are short strings that are added to CSS property names to specify browser-specific implementations. They were introduced to allow browser vendors to experiment with and implement new CSS features before they were standardized. Each browser vendor has its own prefix, such as -webkit- for Chrome and Safari, -moz- for Firefox, and -ms- for Internet Explorer and Microsoft Edge (pre-Chromium version). By using vendor prefixes, developers can target specific browser versions and ensure compatibility with different rendering engines.

- *When to use vendor prefixes*: Vendor prefixes should be used when implementing experimental or nonstandard CSS properties and features that are not fully supported across all browsers. This typically includes cutting-edge features that are still under development or have not yet been standardized by the World Wide Web Consortium (W3C). It is important to note that vendor prefixes should be used only as temporary solutions during the development and testing phase. Once a CSS property or feature becomes widely supported, it is recommended to transition to the standardized version and remove the vendor prefixes.

- *Using vendor prefixes*: When using vendor prefixes, it is crucial to follow best practices to ensure clean and maintainable code. Here are some guidelines to consider:

    a. *Target specific browsers*: Determine which browsers require specific vendor prefixes and apply them selectively. For example, if a particular property requires a prefix for Chrome and Safari, use -webkit-, but exclude other prefixes for browsers that do not need them.

b. *Use the standardized property last*: When including vendor prefixes, always include the standardized property without a prefix last in the declaration block. This ensures that the browser will use the standard version if it supports it, overriding any vendor-prefixed versions.

c. *Include all relevant prefixes*: For better compatibility, it is recommended to include all relevant vendor prefixes for a specific property. This ensures that the property is correctly interpreted by various browsers.

d. *Regularly update prefixes*: Keep track of browser updates and gradually remove vendor prefixes for properties that have become widely supported. This helps to reduce code redundancy and improve performance.

- *Prefix-free solutions*: As browser support for CSS properties and features improves over time, the need for vendor prefixes decreases. It is always recommended to check the current browser support matrix and consider using prefix-free solutions whenever possible. This helps streamline code and reduce maintenance efforts.

In conclusion, vendor prefixes play a crucial role in achieving cross-browser compatibility during the development phase. By using these prefixes strategically and following best practices, front-end developers can ensure that their CSS styles are rendered consistently across different browsers and rendering engines. However, as browser support evolves, it is important to monitor updates and gradually phase out vendor prefixes in favor of standardized CSS properties. This ensures a cleaner codebase and better performance while maintaining compatibility with older browser versions.

```
.round-edge{
    -khtml-border-radius: 10px; /* Konqueror */
    -rim-border-radius: 10px; /* RIM */
     ms border-radius: 10px; /* Microsoft */
    -o-border-radius: 10px; /* Opera */
    -moz-border-radius: 10px; /* Mozilla (e.g Firefox) */
    -webkit-border-radius: 10px; /* Webkit (e.g. Safari and
      Chrome) */
    border-radius: 10px; /* W3C */
}
# Compare and add code and text from book
```

Multiple Columns and Responsive Design in CSS3

Column-based designs have been popular since the time of newspapers, and this continues in the world of the Web. CSS code now will let you arrange your content in columns as opposed to an era where developers needed to define content separately in an element and then style it accordingly. The older code would look something like this:

```
<div id="headlines">
    <p>
        Lorem ipsum dolor sit amet consectetur adipisicing
        elit. Non magni ad qui earum natus aspernatur sequi
        voluptate
        possimus sint praesentium! Natus, ducimus! A velit iste
        cumque placeat ut adipisci et. Lorem, ipsum dolor sit
```

```
    amet consectetur adipisicing elit. Temporibus delectus,
    eligendi maiores aut error perferendis similique.
    Delectus corporis,
    autem temporibus odit officiis unde molestias magnam
    quae vel blanditiis. Illum, quibusdam.
  </p>
  <p>
    Lorem ipsum, dolor sit amet consectetur adipisicing
    elit. Blanditiis rerum ipsam quam quod iure. Aliquam
    provident totam iure
    tempore omnis incidunt aut obcaecati numquam eligendi
    doloremque quibusdam cum, temporibus doloribus. Lorem
    ipsum dolor sit amet
    consectetur adipisicing elit. Provident similique earum
    officia numquam reiciendis sint quod modi sit dolore,
    cumque atque eaque
    suscipit blanditiis assumenda fugiat facere veniam.
    Hic, doloremque.
  </p>
</div>
```

Visual Studio Code provides a way to generate the lorem ipsum text by typing **Lorem** and pressing Enter on autosuggestion.

Let's use the CSS code to make this text flow in a columnar fashion.

```
#headlines {
    column-width: 15em;
}
```

This CSS code will arrange the text in columns no more than 15em wide (see Figure 5-1).

Figure 5-1. *HTML code displaying multiple columns in Chrome browser (desktop)*

The iPad Air will show the content as displayed in Figure 5-2.

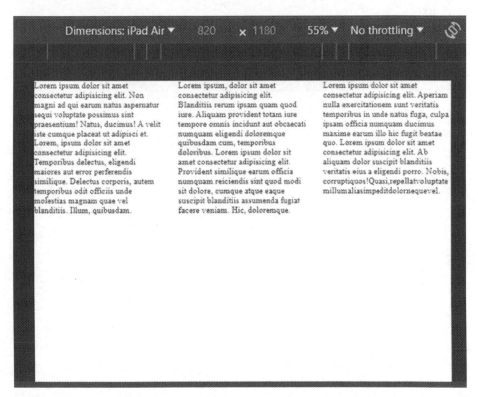

Figure 5-2. *HTML code displaying multiple columns in Chrome browser (iPad Air)*

Beautifying the Column Layout

Adding a gap and column divider is one way to beautify the content in the columns. For that, the CSS changes required are shown here (see Figure 5-3 and Figure 5-4):

```
#headlines {
    column-width: 15em;
    column-rule: thin solid steelblue;
    column-gap: 2em;
}
```

Figure 5-3. *HTML code displaying multiple columns with additional CSS in Chrome browser*

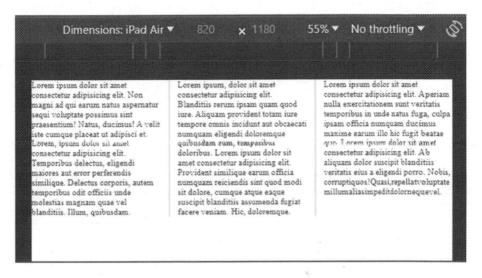

Figure 5-4. *HTML code displaying multiple columns with additional CSS in Chrome browser (iPad Air)*

You can find CSS multicolumn layout specifications at `https://www.w3.org/TR/css-multicol-1/`.

Word Wrapping

In columnar design, there will times when one needs to break a long word onto the next line because it just won't fit in the space available. Without word wrapping, the text will overflow from its allocated space, as shown in Figure 5-5.

Figure 5-5. *HTML code without word wrapping shown in Chrome*

Check the last line of the last column. It is breaking its allocated space and overflowing. CSS provides an easy way to fix this and works well with older versions of browsers as well.

You need to include the following code in your CSS:

```
word-wrap : break-word;
```

This fix looks like Figure 5-6.

Figure 5-6. *HTML code with word wrapping shown in Chrome*

New CSS3 Selectors

Let's now cover the new CSS3 selectors.

The Universal Selector

The universal selector, represented by an asterisk, targets all the elements on a web page. It can be particularly useful for applying global styles or resets across an entire document.

Here is an example:

```
* {
    margin: 0;
    padding: 0;
}
```

Attribute Selectors

CSS3 introduced attribute selectors to allow developers to select elements based on their attributes and attribute values. This gives greater flexibility in styling and targeting specific elements dynamically.

Here is an example:

```css
input[type="text"] {
    background-color: #f2f2f2;
}
```

Negation Selector

The negation selector (:not) enables developers to select elements that do not match a particular selector. It is a powerful tool to override styles or exclude specific elements from a selection.

Here is an example:

```css
p:not(.highlight) {
    color: #333;
}
```

Adjacent Sibling Selector

The adjacent sibling selector (+) targets an element that directly follows another element. This selector is handy when you want to style the element that comes immediately after a specific element.

Here is an example:

```css
h2 + p {
    margin-top: 10px;
}
```

General Sibling Selector

The general sibling selector is similar to the adjacent sibling selector, but it selects all siblings that come after the specified element, not just the immediate one.

Here's an example:

```
h2 ~ p {
    margin-top: 10px;
}
```

First Child Selector

The first child selector (:first-child) selects the first child element of its parent. It is often used to target specific styles to the first element within a container.

Here's an example:

```
li:first-child {
    font-weight: bold;
}
```

Last Child Selector

Similar to the first child selector, the last child selector (:last-child) targets the last child element of its parent.

Here's an example:

```
li:last-child {
    margin-bottom: 10px;
}
```

Empty Selector

The empty selector (:empty) selects elements that have no child elements or text content. It can be used to style elements that do not contain any content.

Here's an example:

```
div:empty {
    display: none;
}
```

Nth Child Selector

The nth child selector (:nth-child) allows developers to select elements based on their position within a parent. It takes an argument in the form of an+b, enabling the precise selection of elements.

Here's an example:

```
li:nth-child(2n) {
    background-color: #f2f2f2;
}
```

Root Selector

The root selector (:root) targets the root element of a document, usually the <html> element. It is useful for applying styles to the entire document.

Here's an example:

```
:root {
    font-size: 16px;
}
```

CSS3 has revolutionized the way web developers style and select elements on web pages. The new selectors introduced in CSS3 offer increased flexibility and control, allowing developers to target elements with precision. By utilizing these selectors effectively, developers can create cleaner, more maintainable code and enhance the user experience. Leveraging the power of these selectors is a valuable skill for any web developer seeking to create modern and visually appealing websites.

CSS3 String Manipulation Attribute Selectors

Let's cover more about selectors. The following section covers how string manipulation can be done using CSSD3, few of the examples could be string matching, partial string matching, prefix or suffix matching.

Attribute Selectors Recap

Before diving into substring matching attribute selectors, let's recap the basics of attribute selectors in CSS3. Attribute selectors allow you to select elements based on their attributes and attribute values. The basic syntax for attribute selectors is as follows:

```
element[attribute="value"] {
    /* Styles to be applied */
}
```

Substring Matching Attribute Selectors

CSS3 introduced four different substring matching attribute selectors that provide varying degrees of flexibility when selecting elements based on attribute values. These selectors are as follows:

- [attribute^="value"] (Prefix match)

- [attribute$="value"] (Suffix match)

- [attribute*="value"] (Substring match)

- [attribute~="value"] (Word match)

Let's explore each selector in detail.

Prefix Match

The prefix match selector ([attribute^="value"]) targets elements whose attribute value begins with a specific value.

Here's an example:

```
a[href^="https://"] {
    /* Styles applied to links with URLs starting with
    "https://" */
}
```

Suffix Match

The suffix match selector ([attribute$="value"]) targets elements whose attribute value ends with a specific value.

Here's an example:

```
img[src$=".png"] {
    /* Styles applied to images with source URLs ending in
    ".png" */
}
```

Substring Match

The substring match selector ([attribute*="value"]) targets elements whose attribute value contains a specific value anywhere within it.

Here's an example:

```
input[type*="email"] {
    /* Styles applied to input fields with a type containing
    the word "email" */
}
```

Word Match

The word match selector ([attribute~="value"]) targets elements whose attribute value contains a specific value as a whole word (separated by spaces).

Here's an example:

```
p[class~="highlight"] {
    /* Styles applied to paragraphs with the class name
    containing the word "highlight" */
}
```

Practical Examples

Let's explore some practical examples to demonstrate the power of substring-matching attribute selectors.

Example 1: Styling External Links

```
a[href^="http://"]:not([href^="https://"]) {
    /* Styles applied to external links (excluding
    "https://") */
    /* e.g., http://example.com */
}
```

Example 2: Targeting File Types

```
a[href$=".pdf"] {
    /* Styles applied to links pointing to PDF files */
}
```

Example 3: Input Validation

```
input[type*="password"]:invalid {
    /* Styles applied to password input fields when they are
    invalid */
}
```

Example 4: Styling Tags with Specific Classes

```
div[class~="important"] {
    /* Styles applied to div elements with the class name
    containing the word "important" */
}
```

CSS3 substring matching attribute selectors provide web developers with a powerful toolset to select elements based on specific attribute values. By using these selectors effectively, you can apply targeted styles to elements, resulting in enhanced user experiences and improved design aesthetics. Understanding and harnessing the potential of substring matching attribute selectors will enable you to create more dynamic and visually appealing websites. Experiment with these selectors and unlock their potential to take your CSS skills to new heights.

Custom Web Typography

Web typography plays a crucial role in creating engaging and visually appealing websites. It goes beyond mere content presentation and serves as an art form that can enhance user experience, establish branding, and convey the desired tone and mood. With the advancements in CSS3, designers now have more power and flexibility to unleash their creativity and create stunning custom typography on the Web. In this section, we will delve into the world of custom web typography in CSS3, exploring the techniques and features that allow designers to push the boundaries of typographic design.

Web Fonts

One of the fundamental components of custom web typography is the use of web fonts. CSS3 provides support for embedding custom fonts using the @font-face rule. This allows designers to include unique typefaces that aren't commonly available on users' systems. By incorporating custom web fonts, designers can align their typography with the overall design concept, creating a more cohesive and personalized user experience.

Font Stacks

Font stacks are a collection of fallback fonts specified in CSS. These stacks ensure that if a particular font is not available, the browser automatically selects the next available font from the stack. With CSS3, designers can create font stacks that include custom web fonts, system fonts, and even fallbacks from popular font families. This ensures consistent typography across different devices and platforms while still preserving the intended visual aesthetic.

Text Effects and Decorations

CSS3 introduces various properties that enable designers to apply creative effects and decorations to their typography. Some of these properties include text-shadow, text-stroke, text-underline-offset, and text-decoration-style. These features allow designers to add shadows, strokes, and unique decorations to the text, making it stand out and capturing users' attention. Customizing these properties creatively can help emphasize important elements, highlight headings, or create visual hierarchy within the content.

Variable Fonts

CSS3 brings the exciting concept of variable fonts, which are font files that contain multiple variations within a single file. These variations can include different weights, styles, and even width adjustments. By utilizing variable fonts, designers can achieve greater flexibility in customizing typography, allowing for smooth transitions between font styles and seamless responsiveness across different screen sizes. This enables the creation of unique typographic designs that adapt to the needs of the content and the device it is displayed on.

Animations and Transitions

CSS3 transitions and animations provide a powerful toolset for bringing typography to life on the Web. By applying transition or animation properties to text elements, designers can introduce dynamic effects, such as fading, scaling, rotating, or even moving characters. These techniques can be used sparingly to add subtle motion to headlines or creatively to create eye-catching typographic animations. When used thoughtfully, animations and transitions can greatly enhance the user experience and make the typography more engaging and memorable.

Custom web typography in CSS3 allows designers to break free from the limitations of standard system fonts and unleash their creativity in crafting captivating and unique typographic designs. With the ability to embed custom web fonts, utilize font stacks, apply text effects and decorations, leverage variable fonts, and incorporate animations and transitions, designers can create web experiences that are visually stunning, on brand, and highly engaging. By embracing the art of custom web typography, designers can elevate the overall aesthetics of their websites and leave a lasting impression on users.

@font-face Typography in Responsive Design

In today's digital landscape, responsive design has become crucial to ensure a seamless user experience across devices of various sizes and resolutions. Typography plays a vital role in web design, and with the @ font-face rule in CSS, designers can now incorporate custom fonts to enhance the visual appeal of their websites. In this section, we will explore how @font-face typography can be effectively utilized in responsive design, along with practical examples.

Font Selection

When considering the @font-face typography for responsive design, it is essential to choose fonts that are legible and visually appealing across different screen sizes. Opt for fonts that offer a variety of weights and styles to allow flexibility in adjusting the typography for different contexts. For example, a font like Open Sans provides various weights, allowing designers to adapt the font to different device resolutions seamlessly.

Here's an example:

```
@font-face {
    font-family: 'Open Sans';
    src: url('open-sans-regular.woff2') format('woff2'),
         url('open-sans-regular.woff') format('woff');
    font-weight: normal;
    font-style: normal;
}
```

Font Formats

To ensure compatibility across different browsers and devices, include font files in multiple formats, such as TrueType (.ttf), OpenType (.otf), Web Open Font Format (.woff), and Web Open Font Format 2.0 (.woff2). This allows the browser to select the appropriate format based on its capabilities, ensuring that the custom font is displayed correctly.

Here's an example:

```
@font-face {
    font-family: 'Open Sans';
    src: url('open-sans-regular.woff2') format('woff2'),
        url('open-sans-regular.woff') format('woff'),
        url('open-sans-regular.ttf') format('truetype');
    font-weight: normal;
    font-style: normal;
}
```

Media Queries

Media queries are essential for adapting typography to different screen sizes and devices in responsive design. By using media queries, designers can adjust font sizes, line heights, and other typographic properties based on the viewport dimensions.

Here's an example:

```
@media screen and (max-width: 768px) {
    body {
        font-size: 16px;
    }
}
```

145

Fluid Typography

Fluid typography ensures that font sizes and other typographic properties scale smoothly with the viewport size. This technique maintains optimal readability and aesthetics across different devices.

Here's an example:

```
@media screen and (max-width: 768px) {
    body {
      font-size: calc(14px + 2vw);
    }
}
```

Performance Optimization

To optimize font loading and page performance, designers can implement techniques such as font subsetting, font preloading, and asynchronous font loading. These techniques help reduce page load times, particularly on mobile devices with limited bandwidth.

Here's an example:

```
<link rel="preload" href="open-sans-regular.woff2" as="font"
type="font/woff2" crossorigin="anonymous">
```

@FontFace typography in responsive design offers designers the flexibility to incorporate custom fonts while ensuring optimal legibility and aesthetics across different devices. By carefully selecting fonts, utilizing appropriate font formats, leveraging media queries for responsive adjustments, implementing fluid typography techniques, and optimizing font loading, designers can create visually stunning and user-friendly websites. Embrace @font-face typography in your responsive design practices to enhance the overall typography and elevate the user experience.

CSS3 Color Formats

Colors play a crucial role in web design, setting the mood, conveying information, and capturing users' attention. CSS3 introduced new color formats that offer greater flexibility and expressiveness for designers. In this section, we will explore some of the new CSS3 color formats and provide code examples to showcase their usage and advantages in web design.

RGBA and HSLA

Red Green Blue Alpha (RGBA) and Hue Saturation Lightness Alpha (HSLA) are color formats that allow designers to specify transparency or opacity levels for colors. These formats are particularly useful for creating subtle gradients, overlays, and blending effects.

Here are some code examples:

/* **RGBA** */

```
background-color: rgba(255, 0, 0, 0.5); /* Semi-transparent red
background */
```

/* **HSLA** */

```
color: hsla(240, 100%, 50%, 0.8); /* Semi-transparent
blue text */
```

HEX with Alpha Channel

CSS3 introduced the ability to specify an alpha channel for hex color values. The alpha channel controls the transparency level of the color, allowing for versatile opacity adjustments.

Here are some code examples:

```
background-color: #ff000080; /* Semi-transparent red
background */
```

CSS Named Colors

CSS3 expanded the list of named colors, providing a broader range of predefined color values that designers can use directly in their CSS code. This simplifies the process of color selection and allows for consistent color usage across different projects.

Here is a code example:

```
color: papayawhip; /* Set text color to 'Papaya Whip' */
```

Hue Saturation Lightness

HSL is a color format that allows designers to define colors based on their hue, saturation, and lightness. This format provides greater control over color variations and makes it easier to create harmonious color schemes.

Here is a code example:

```
background-color: hsl(120, 100%, 50%); /* Set background color
to a vibrant green */
```

RGB with Percentage

In addition to the traditional RGB color format using integer values (0–255), CSS3 introduced the option to specify RGB values using percentages. This allows for more flexible and intuitive color manipulation.

Here is a code example:

```
color: rgb(50%, 0%, 75%); /* Set text color to a
purplish hue */
```

Transparent

CSS3 introduced the transparent keyword, which allows designers to create fully transparent elements. This is particularly useful when creating layered effects or overlays.

Here is a code example:

```
background-color: transparent; /* Create a fully transparent
background */
```

Most of the IDEs provide their own color picker with RGB and hex values. Figure 5-7 shows the Visual Studio Code editor, which shows only RGB values on the top heading.

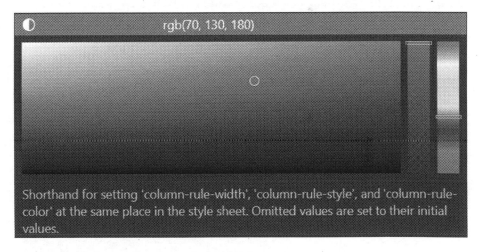

Figure 5-7. *Visual Studio Color picker*

The new CSS3 color formats provide designers with enhanced flexibility, expressiveness, and ease of use in web design. RGBA and HSLA allow for transparent color definitions, hex with alpha channel enables opacity adjustments, CSS named colors simplify color selection, HSL provides granular control over color variations, RGB with percentage offers intuitive color manipulation, and the transparent keyword facilitates the creation of layered effects. By incorporating these new color formats into their CSS code, designers can create visually captivating and dynamic web designs that effectively convey their intended message.

Summary

This chapter focused on the CSS selectors, color modes, and different ways the same color can be defined and interpreted by Cascading Style Sheets. The chapter started by exploring the power of CSS3 and understanding the building blocks of CSS3 such as selectors, properties, values, and declarations. It also covered the specific browser vendors' related prefixes, how multiple columns can be created, and how to resolve the flow of the longer words in columns. The chapter explained the new CSS selectors and how CSS3 string manipulation works. We then covered custom web typography followed by the @font-face typography. The last topic for this chapter was CSS color formats.

CHAPTER 6

Animations and Transitions in CSS3

Animation is a new and promising feature in CSS and used to communicate or promote various visual aids. This chapter focuses on how to create animations using CSS3. It covers animating text content, along with the properties you need and how the browser will display it. It then covers animating objects. Next the chapter covers CSS transitions and the attributes required to create those transitions. The last two topics are 2D and 3D transformations.

Animating with CSS3

Prior to CSS3, Adobe Flash was used to include animations on a web page. Any prior experience in Flash can be used to work with CSS3 animations, which employs keyframing conventions similar to Flash.

To create CSS3 animations, first you create the keyframes declaration, and second you use the keyframe in the animation property.

The keyframe declaration looks like this:

```
@keyframes slide-in {
      from { opacity: 0; transform: translateX(-100px); }
      to { opacity: 1; transform: translateX(0); }
    }
```

© Varun Gor 2023
V. Gor, *Creating Responsive Websites Using HTML5 and CSS3*,
https://doi.org/10.1007/978-1-4842-9783-4_6

Using the defined keyframe in the animation property looks like this:

```
.element {
        animation-name: slide-in;
        animation-duration: 1s;
        animation-timing-function: ease-in-out;
        animation-delay: 1s;
        animation-iteration-count: infinite;
        animation-fill-mode: forwards;
        color: #d42e2e;
        align-self: center;
    }
```

Figure 6-1 shows how the browser will display the text or image animated a movement from left to right.

Content sliding from Left to Right

Figure 6-1. *HTML code displaying text animation in Chrome*

What Are the Animation Properties?

Table 6-1 describes the animation properties and their usage.

Table 6-1. *Animation Properties and Their Meaning*

Property	Usage
@keyframe	This is used to specify the animation (along with its name).
animation-name	This is used to define the animation using @keyframe that will be used in CSS.
animation-duration	This specifies the time animation takes to complete one cycle.
animation-timing-function	This specifies the speed curve of the animation.
animation-delay	This specifies the time when the animation will start.
animation-iteration-count	This specifies the number of times animation is repeated.
animation-fill-mode	This specifies the style of the element when animation is not played.
animation-direction	This specifies how the animation should be played, in reverse or alternate cycles.
animation-play-state	This specifies the current play state of the animation, such as playing or paused.

Animating an Object

Let's look at another code example where an object is moving from left to right and from the bottom up and then comes back to its original position. At the same time it is changing colors.

Here is the CSS code:

```
div {
        width: 150px;
        height: 150px;
        position: relative;
        background: teal;
        -webkit-animation: second 7s; /* Chrome, Safari, Opera */
        animation: second 7s;
    }
```

Here is the animation code:

```
/* Standard syntax */
    @keyframes second {
        0%   {background:teal; left:0px; top:0px;}
        25%  {background:turquoise; left:300px; top:0px;}
        50%  {background:seagreen; left:300px; top:200px;}
        75%  {background:saddlebrown; left:0px; top:200px;}
        100% {background:teal; left:0px; top:0px;}
    }
```

Now all that is required is to place a <div> tag in the HTML file and load it into any modern browser. It should display something like Figure 6-2.

Figure 6-2. *HTML code displaying animated objects in Chrome*

CSS3 Transitions

Web design is all about creating captivating user experiences, and CSS3 transitions offer a powerful tool for adding smooth and elegant animations to your web pages. With CSS3 transitions, developers can easily animate changes in CSS property values, such as color, size, position, and opacity, creating visually appealing and interactive elements. In this section, we will explore the versatility of CSS3 transitions and their key concepts and provide a comprehensive guide on how to implement them effectively in your web designs.

Understanding CSS3 Transitions

CSS3 transitions enable developers to create animated transitions between two states of an element. By specifying the starting and ending property values and defining the duration and timing function, CSS3 transitions smoothly interpolate the property changes, resulting in a visually pleasing animation. Unlike CSS3 animations that require keyframes and explicit control over intermediate states, transitions automatically handle the intermediate stages, making them ideal for simple and straightforward animations.

Key Concepts of CSS3 Transitions

Here are the key concepts of CSS3 transitions:

- *Transition property*: The transition property specifies which CSS properties should be animated and the duration of the transition. For example, transition: width 1s will animate changes to the width property over a one-second duration.

155

- *Transition timing function*: The transition-timing-function property determines the rate of change during the transition. CSS3 provides various timing functions, including linear, ease, ease-in, ease-out, and ease-in-out, each offering a distinct acceleration and deceleration effect.

- *Transition duration*: The transition-duration property sets the time it takes for the transition to complete. You can specify the duration in seconds (s) or milliseconds (ms). For example, transition-duration: 0.5s will make the transition last for half a second.

- *Transition delay*: The transition-delay property allows you to introduce a delay before the transition begins. This can be useful for staggering multiple transitions or creating a delayed effect.

Implementing CSS3 Transitions

Let's explore a step-by-step guide to implementing CSS3 transitions effectively.

Step 1: Choose the Target Element

Identify the element you want to animate and ensure it has a defined starting state. For example, let's use a <button> element with a background color.

Step 2: Define the Transition

Specify the transition property on the element, setting the desired properties to animate, their durations, and timing functions. For example:

```
button {
    transition: background-color 0.3s ease-in-out;
}
```

Step 3: Trigger the Transition

Apply a CSS state change to the element, such as hovering over it, clicking it, or adding/removing a class. For example:

```
button:hover {
    background-color: #ff0000;
}
```

Step 4: Customize and Experiment

Fine-tune your transitions by adjusting the timing functions, durations, and other properties. Experiment with different properties and combinations to create unique effects.

CSS3 transitions empower web developers to add fluid and engaging animations to their designs effortlessly. By leveraging the transition property along with timing functions, durations, and delays, you can create visually stunning effects that enhance the user experience. Whether it's a subtle fade-in, a smooth color transition, or an animated transformation, CSS3 transitions offer endless possibilities for elevating your web designs. So, go ahead, unleash your creativity, and harness the power of CSS3 transitions to captivate your audience and make your web pages come alive.

The browser will display the HTML page without hovering over the button (see Figure 6-3).

Figure 6-3. *HTML code displaying a transition in Chrome (without mouse hover)*

The browser will display the HTML page when the mouse hovers over the button (see Figure 6-4).

Figure 6-4. *HTML code displaying a transition in Chrome (with mouse hover)*

The Properties of Transition

In CSS3, transition properties allow you to create smooth and animated transitions between different states of an element. They enable you to define how specific CSS properties change over time, resulting in visually appealing animations. CSS3 provides several transition properties to control various aspects of the animation process. Let's explore the most important transition properties in CSS3.

transition-property

The transition-property property specifies the CSS properties you want to animate. You can specify multiple properties separated by commas or use the value all to animate all the applicable properties. For example:

```
.element {
        transition-property: width, opacity;
}
```

In this example, changes to the width and opacity properties of the element will be animated.

transition-duration

The transition-duration property sets the duration over which the transition occurs. It determines how long it takes for the transition to complete, and it accepts time values in seconds (s) or milliseconds (ms). For example:

```
.element {
        transition-duration: 0.5s;
}
```

This specifies that the transition should take half a second to complete.

transition-timing-function

The transition-timing-function property controls the pace of the transition. It determines how the intermediate property values are calculated over time. CSS3 provides several predefined timing functions, including the following:

- *linear*: Produces a constant transition speed

- *ease*: Starts slowly, accelerates in the middle, and slows down again toward the end

- *ease-in*: Starts slowly and accelerates toward the end

- *ease-out*: Starts quickly and decelerates toward the end

- *ease-in-out*: Starts slowly, accelerates in the middle, and decelerates toward the end

You can also use the cubic-bezier() function to create custom timing functions. For example:

```
.element {
        transition-timing-function: ease-in-out;
}
```

This specifies that the transition should have an easing effect.

transition-delay

The transition-delay property introduces a delay before the transition starts. It allows you to control when the transition should begin after a state change. You can specify the delay using time values in seconds (s) or milliseconds (ms). For example:

```
.element {
      transition-delay: 0.2s;
}
```

This adds a 0.2-second delay before the transition starts.

By combining these transition properties, you can create dynamic and engaging animations in your CSS3 stylesheets. Experimenting with different values for these properties enables you to achieve the desired effects, such as smooth fades, sliding transitions, or transformations.

The Transition Shorthand Property

In CSS3, you can use shorthand properties to define multiple transition-related properties at once. These shorthand properties provide a convenient way to specify the transition property, duration, timing function, and delay in a single declaration. The following are the shorthand properties available for transitions in CSS3.

transition

The transition shorthand property allows you to specify the transition property, duration, timing function, and delay in a single line. The values are specified in the following order: transition-property, transition-duration, transition-timing-function, and transition-delay. Here's an example:

```
.element {
  transition: width 0.5s ease-in-out 0.2s;
}
```

In this example, the width property will transition over a duration of 0.5 seconds, with an easing effect using the ease-in-out timing function, and a delay of 0.2 seconds.

transition-property

The transition-property shorthand property allows you to specify multiple properties to be transitioned. You can separate the property names using commas. For example:

```
.element {
  transition-property: width, height, opacity;
}
```

In this example, changes to the width, height, and opacity properties will be animated.

transition-duration

The transition-duration shorthand property allows you to specify the duration for multiple transitions. You can provide multiple time values separated by commas. For example:

```
.element {
  transition-duration: 0.5s, 1s, 0.3s;
}
```

In this example, each transition will have a different duration: 0.5 seconds, 1 second, and 0.3 seconds.

transition-timing-function

The transition-timing-function shorthand property allows you to specify the timing functions for multiple transitions. You can provide multiple timing function values separated by commas. For example:

```
.element {
  transition-timing-function: ease-in-out, linear, ease-in;
}
```

In this example, each transition will have a different timing function applied.

transition-delay

The transition-delay shorthand property allows you to specify the delay for multiple transitions. You can provide multiple time values separated by commas. For example:

```
.element {
  transition-delay: 0.2s, 0.5s, 0s;
}
```

In this example, each transition will have a different delay: 0.2 seconds, 0.5 seconds, and no delay (0 seconds).

By using these shorthand properties, you can easily and efficiently define multiple transition-related values, making your CSS code more concise and readable. Remember to experiment with different values to achieve the desired effects for your transitions.

Understanding Timing Functions

CSS3 transitions offer a powerful way to animate changes in CSS properties, providing smooth and visually appealing transitions between different states. One crucial aspect of CSS3 transitions is the timing function, which controls the rate of change during the transition. By understanding and leveraging timing functions, web developers can add depth and personality to their animations. In this article, we will explore the various timing functions available in CSS3 transitions and delve into their effects on the animation process.

The Basics of Timing Functions

A timing function defines how intermediate property values are calculated over time during a CSS3 transition. It influences the acceleration and deceleration of the animation, creating distinct visual effects. CSS3 provides several predefined timing functions and even allows developers to create custom functions using the cubic-bezier() function.

Common Timing Functions

Here are the custom timing functions.

linear

The linear timing function produces a constant transition speed throughout the animation. It creates a linear progression without any acceleration or deceleration. This function is suitable for animations requiring a consistent speed. For example:

```
transition-timing-function: linear;
```

ease

The ease timing function is the default in CSS3 transitions. It starts slowly, accelerates in the middle, and slows down toward the end. The ease function adds a subtle easing effect, providing a more natural and pleasing animation. For example:

```
transition-timing-function: ease;
```

ease-in

The ease-in timing function starts slowly and accelerates toward the end. It produces a smooth and gentle entrance, perfect for transitions that emphasize the beginning. For example:

```
transition-timing-function: ease-in;
```

ease-out

The ease-out timing function starts quickly and decelerates toward the end. It creates a smooth and gradual exit, often used to highlight the end of a transition. For example:

```
transition-timing-function: ease-out;
```

ease-in-out

The ease-in-out timing function combines the characteristics of ease-in and ease-out. It starts slowly, accelerates in the middle, and decelerates toward the end. This timing function provides a balanced effect suitable for a wide range of transitions. For example:

```
transition-timing-function: ease-in-out;
```

Creating Custom Timing Functions

CSS3 also allows developers to create custom timing functions using the cubic-bezier() function. This function accepts four values ranging from 0 to 1, specifying the x and y coordinates of the control points on a cubic Bézier curve. By adjusting these values, developers can achieve unique and tailored easing effects. For example:

```
transition-timing-function: cubic-bezier(0.42, 0, 0.58, 1);
```

Experimentation and Fine-Tuning

To determine the best timing function for your transitions, it's essential to experiment and fine-tune the effects. Consider the context, the desired animation style, and the emotional impact you want to convey. Test different timing functions with your transitions and observe the changes in acceleration and deceleration to find the most suitable one.

Timing functions in CSS3 transitions play a significant role in creating captivating and engaging animations. By understanding the different timing functions available, developers can breathe life into their transitions, adding depth, personality, and impact. Whether it's the simplicity of linear transitions, the naturalness of ease functions, or the customizability of cubic Bézier curves, timing functions empower web developers to create memorable user experiences. So, dive into the world of timing functions, experiment, and let your transitions come alive with CSS3's incredible possibilities.

CSS3 2D Transitions

CSS3 offers a wide range of powerful tools to bring creativity and interactivity to web design. Among these tools, 2D transformations provide the ability to manipulate elements in two-dimensional space, allowing for visually stunning effects and engaging user experiences. In this section, we will delve into the world of CSS3 2D transformations, exploring their capabilities and demonstrating how they can be used to bring life and dynamism to web pages.

Understanding CSS3 2D Transformations

CSS3 2D transformations enable developers to modify the position, size, rotation, and skew of elements in a two-dimensional space. These transformations offer a flexible way to create captivating effects without the need for complex JavaScript code or external libraries. The key components of CSS3 2D transformations include translation, scaling, rotation, skewing, and origin manipulation.

Translation

Translation allows elements to be moved or shifted along the horizontal and vertical axes. This can be achieved using the translate() function, specifying the distance to move in each direction. For example:

```
.element {
  transform: translate(50px, 20px);
}
```

This will move the element 50 pixels to the right and 20 pixels down.

Scaling

Scaling allows elements to be resized larger or smaller. The scale() function can be used to define the scaling factors for the width and height of an element. For example:

```
.element {
  transform: scale(1.2);
}
```

This will increase the size of the element by 20 percent.

Rotation

Rotation enables elements to be rotated around a specified point. The rotate() function defines the angle of rotation in degrees. For example:

```
.element {
  transform: rotate(45deg);
}
```

This will rotate the element 45 degrees clockwise.

Skewing

Skewing allows elements to be distorted along the horizontal or vertical axis. The skew() function sets the angles of skew in degrees. For example:

```
.element {
  transform: skew(10deg, -5deg);
}
```

This will skew the element 10 degrees horizontally and -5 degrees vertically.

Origin Manipulation

The transformation origin specifies the point around which transformations are applied. By default, the origin is set to the center of the element. However, it can be customized using the transform-origin property. For example:

```
.element {
  transform-origin: top left;
}
```

This will set the transformation origin to the top-left corner of the element.

Combining Transformations

Multiple transformations can be combined to achieve complex effects. Each transformation is applied in the order they are specified. For example:

```
.element {
  transform: translate(50px, 50px) rotate(45deg) scale(1.2);
}
```

This will first translate the element, then rotate it, and finally scale it.

CSS3 2D transformations provide a powerful toolkit for creating visually engaging web experiences. By leveraging translation, scaling, rotation, skewing, and origin manipulation, developers can transform elements, adding depth, motion, and interactivity to their designs. Whether it's animating a navigation menu, creating a playful hover effect, or adding a unique perspective to images, CSS3 2D transformations allow for limitless creativity and innovation. So, embrace the power of CSS3 2D transformations, experiment, and let your web designs come to life with captivating transformations.

CSS3 3D Transformations

In the realm of modern web design, creating visually captivating and interactive experiences is a top priority. CSS3 offers a powerful set of tools to bring designs to life, and one such tool is CSS3 3D transformations. With CSS3 3D transformations, developers can manipulate elements in three-dimensional space, allowing for stunning and immersive effects. In this section, we will explore the world of CSS3 3D transformations, understanding their concepts and discovering how they can take web design to the next level.

Understanding CSS3 3D Transformations

CSS3 3D transformations enable developers to manipulate elements in a three-dimensional space, adding depth, perspective, and realism to web pages. These transformations allow for the rotation, scaling, translation, and skewing of elements along the x-, y-, and z-axes. By combining these transformations, developers can create impressive 3D effects, animations, and interactions.

Key Concepts of CSS3 3D Transformations

Here are the key concepts of CSS3 3D transformations.

Perspective

Perspective is a critical concept in CSS3 3D transformations. It establishes the depth and viewing perspective for the 3D space. By applying the perspective property to a parent element, you define the distance at which the viewer perceives the 3D space. This property creates a sense of depth and realism.

169

Transformations in 3D Space

CSS3 3D transformations provide a range of properties to manipulate elements in three-dimensional space.

- rotateX(), rotateY(), rotateZ(): These properties rotate an element around the x-, y-, or z-axes, respectively.

- scale3d(): This property scales an element along all three axes.

- translate3d(): This property moves an element in three-dimensional space, allowing for translations along the x-, y-, or z-axes.

- skewX(), skewY(): These properties skew an element along the x- or y-axis.

Combining Transformations

Developers can combine multiple transformations to achieve complex 3D effects. By applying different rotation, scaling, translation, and skewing properties, elements can be transformed in unique and captivating ways. Experimentation and fine-tuning are key to achieving desired results.

Implementing CSS3 3D Transformations

Let's explore a step-by-step guide on how to implement CSS3 3D transformations effectively.

Setting the Perspective

Apply perspective to the parent element using the perspective property. This establishes the depth and viewing perspective for the 3D space. For example:

```
.container {
  perspective: 800px;
}
```

Defining 3D Transformations

Apply 3D transformations to the target elements using the appropriate transformation properties. These transformations manipulate elements in three-dimensional space. For example:

```
.element {
  transform: rotateY(45deg) translateZ(100px);
}
```

Combining and Experimenting

Combine multiple transformation properties to create captivating 3D effects. Experiment with different rotation angles, scaling factors, translation distances, and skewing values to achieve the desired visual impact. Fine-tune the transformations to achieve seamless and engaging animations.

CSS3 3D transformations open up a world of creative possibilities for web designers and developers. By harnessing the power of perspective, rotation, scaling, translation, and skewing in three-dimensional space, developers can create visually stunning and immersive web experiences. Whether it's creating 3D carousels, flipping cards, parallax scrolling effects, or interactive 3D menus, CSS3 3D transformations offer endless opportunities to captivate users and elevate web design. So, embrace the power of CSS3 3D transformations, experiment, and let your creativity soar in the realm of three-dimensional web experiences.

Summary

This chapter covered animations, animation properties, and transitions and showed how to implement a simple CSS transition. This chapter also covered the transition shorthand property along with the timing functions. The chapter explained how to create a custom timing function with a code example. Following this, the chapter explained CSS 2D and 3D transformations.

CHAPTER 7

Background and Shadows in CSS

This chapter covers the shadow effect using CSS. The first topic covered is text shadows. We'll talk about how to add shadows to text to make it more attractive, what color and how color palletes can be applied, and what the properties of the shadows are. It also explains how to prevent text shadows using CSS. Another amazing feature that will be covered is the embossed text shadow effect. We'll also cover box shadows, background gradients, and more.

Text Shadows with CSS3

One of the most attractive features of any website is its content, and text shadows make it look serene. With CSS3, they are even easier to implement. This feature text-shadow is widely supported by many of the modern browsers.

Here is some example code:

```
.text {
    text-shadow: 2px 2px 2px #ff0000;
}
```

© Varun Gor 2023
V. Gor, *Creating Responsive Websites Using HTML5 and CSS3*,
https://doi.org/10.1007/978-1-4842-9783-4_7

Let's try to understand what this syntax means. As per the rule values, the shorthand rules go right and then down. Hence, the first 2px value represents the shadow to the right, followed by the 2px value representing the shadow down, and the next 2px value represents the blur. Lastly, the color of the shadow is specified (it can be in hex, HSL, or RGB).

Let's consider the following code example to see how text-shadow works.

Here is the HTML file:

```
<!DOCTYPE html>
<html>
<head>
  <title>Text Shadow Using CSS3</title>
  <style>
    .shadow-text {
      font-size: 36px;
      font-weight: bold;
      text-shadow: 2px 2px 4px #e32a2a;
    }
  </style>
</head>
<body>
  <h1 class="shadow-text">Hello, World!</h1>
</body>
</html>
```

Figure 7-1 shows what this looks like in a browser.

Hello, World!

Figure 7-1. *HTML displaying text shadow in Chrome*

Allowed Color Values

It is not necessary to define the shadow color in hex values; the other alternatives are HSL(A) or RGB(A).

If you change the color in the text-shadow definition in the previous code to the one shown here, it will work similar to the one defined earlier:

```
text-shadow: 2px 2px 4px hsla(0, 77%, 53%, 1);
```

The following is its equivalent RGB definition:

```
text-shadow: 2px 2px 4px rgb(227, 42, 42);
```

As observed, the value for the shadow's horizontal and vertical display goes to the right and down. What if you need to shadow the text to the left and up? It is a simple process. Provide a negative value to the first two attributes, as shown in the following code:

```
<!DOCTYPE html>
<html>
<head>
  <title>Text Shadow Using CSS3</title>
  <style>
    .shadow-text {
      font-size: 36px;
      font-weight: bold;
      text-shadow: -2px -2px 4px rgb(227, 42, 42);

    }
  </style>
</head>
<body>
  <h1 class="shadow-text">Hello, World!</h1>
</body>
</html>
```

Figure 7-2 shows what it looks like in a browser.

Hello, World!

Figure 7-2. *HTML displaying text shadow in Chrome (alternate way of declaring colors)*

How to Prevent a Text Shadow

To prevent the text shadow, the value of text-shadow needs to be changed to none to make the shadow disappear.

Here is the code:

```
<!DOCTYPE html>
<html>
<head>
  <title>Text Shadow Using CSS3</title>
  <style>
    .shadow-text {
      font-size: 36px;
      font-weight: bold;
      text-shadow: none;

    }
  </style>
</head>
<body>
  <h1 class="shadow-text">Hello, World!</h1>
</body>
</html>
```

Figure 7-3 shows what it looks like in a browser.

Hello, World!

Figure 7-3. *HTML displaying how to prevent a text shadow in Chrome*

An Embossed Text Shadow Effect

Creating an embossed text shadow effect using CSS3 involves combining the CSS text-shadow and box-shadow properties. The idea is to create two layers of shadows, one lighter and one darker, to simulate the appearance of the text being embossed.

Here is the HTML:

```
<!DOCTYPE html>
<html lang="en">
<head>
  <meta charset="UTF-8">
  <meta name="viewport" content="width=device-width, initial-
  scale=1.0">
  <title>Embossed Text Shadow</title>
  <style>
    .embossed-text {
      font-size: 48px;
      text-align: center;
      color: #dad4d4; /* Set the text color */
      text-shadow: 1px 1px 0 #262525, -1px -1px 0 #666;
      /*
        The text-shadow property takes a comma-separated list
        of shadows.
```

```
    Each shadow is defined by its horizontal offset,
    vertical offset, blur radius, and color.
    Here, we're creating two shadows: one lighter and
    one darker.
    The positive values (1px) create the lighter
    shadow, and the negative values (-1px) create the
    darker shadow.
    You can adjust the values as needed to get the
    desired effect.
    */

    background-color: #333; /* Set the background color */
    padding: 20px;
    box-shadow: 0 4px 8px rgba(0, 0, 0, 0.3);
    /*
    The box-shadow property creates a shadow around the
    text element to give it depth.
    You can adjust the values to control the shadow's
    spread, blur radius, and opacity.
    */
  }
  </style>
</head>
<body>
  <div class="embossed-text">Embossed Text</div>
</body>
</html>
```

In this example, we have a <div> with the class embossed-text that
represents the text to which we want to apply the embossed effect. The CSS
styles target this class to create the desired effect.

1. Set the font-size, text-align, and color properties for
    the text.

2. Set the text-shadow property to create two shadows
    with a slight offset and no blur. The positive values
    create the lighter shadow (top-right), and the
    negative values create the darker shadow (bottom-
    left). The color of the shadows is defined as #ccc
    (light gray) and #666 (dark gray), respectively.

3. Set the background color of the container to serve as
    the base color for the text.

4. Use the box-shadow property to create a drop
    shadow around the text element, providing a sense
    of depth.

Feel free to adjust the values of the text-shadow and box-shadow
properties to get the desired level of embossed effect for your text.

Multiple Text Shadows

Creating multiple text shadows in CSS3 is easy and allows you to add
interesting and creative effects to your text. You can apply as many
shadows as you want by separating them with commas within the text-
shadow property. Each shadow you define will be layered on top of the
previous one, giving you a wide range of possibilities. Let's look at an
example of how you can create multiple text shadows.

Here is the HTML:

```
<!DOCTYPE html>
<html lang="en">
<head>
  <meta charset="UTF-8">
```

```
<meta name="viewport" content="width=device-width, initial-
scale=1.0">
<title>Multiple Text Shadows</title>
<style>
  .shadow-text {
    font-size: 48px;
    text-align: center;
    color: #fff;
    text-shadow:
      2px 2px 0 #FF0000, /* Red shadow */
      -2px -2px 0 #00FF00, /* Green shadow */
      4px 4px 0 #0000FF; /* Blue shadow */
    /*
      Here, we define three shadows with different colors
      (red, green, and blue) and offsets.
      The positive values (2px and 4px) create the shadows to
      the bottom-right, and the negative values (-2px) create
      shadows to the top-left.
      The blur radius is set to 0, which means no blur is
      applied to the shadows.
    */

    background-color: #333;
    padding: 20px;
  }
</style>
</head>
<body>
  <div class="shadow-text">Multiple Text Shadows</div>
</body>
</html>
```

In this example, we have a <div> with the class shadow-text that represents the text to which we want to apply multiple shadows. The CSS styles target this class to create the desired effect.

1. Set the font-size, text-align, and color properties for the text.

2. Set the text-shadow property with three shadows separated by commas. Each shadow is defined by its horizontal offset, vertical offset, blur radius, and color.

3. Set the background color of the container to serve as the base color for the text.

You can add as many shadows as you want, and you're not limited to just using different colors. You can experiment with various offsets, blur radii, and colors to create unique and visually appealing effects for your text.

Figure 7-4 shows what this looks like in a browser.

Multiple Text Shadows

Figure 7-4. *HTML displaying multiple text shadow in Chrome*

Box Shadows

CSS3 brought a plethora of new possibilities for web designers and developers to create eye-catching and dynamic user interfaces. One of the most versatile and powerful features introduced in CSS3 is the box-shadow property. With box-shadow, designers can add depth, dimension, and visual interest to elements on their web pages, creating a more engaging user experience. In this section, we will explore the box-shadow property in CSS3 and learn how to wield it effectively to enhance your designs.

Understanding the box-shadow Property

The box-shadow property allows you to create one or more shadows for an element, which are typically cast by a light source from above and to the left of the element. The property takes a comma-separated list of shadow values, each defined by four components.

- *Horizontal offset (required)*: This value specifies how far to the right or left the shadow should be offset from the element. Positive values move the shadow to the right, while negative values move it to the left.

- *Vertical offset (required)*: This value determines how far the shadow should be offset from the element vertically. Positive values move the shadow downward, while negative values move it upward.

- *Blur radius (optional)*: The blur radius controls the blurriness of the shadow. Higher values result in a more blurred shadow, while a value of 0 creates a sharp-edged shadow.

- *Spread distance (optional)*: The spread distance expands or contracts the size of the shadow. Positive values increase the size, while negative values shrink it. If not specified, the shadow is the same size as the element.

- *Color (required)*: This value sets the color of the shadow, which can be specified in various formats, such as named colors, hex codes, or RGBa.

Basic Box Shadows

Let's start with some examples of basic box shadows to understand how the box-shadow property works.

Here is the CSS:

```css
/* Example 1: Simple shadow with default values */
.box {
    box-shadow: 3px 3px 5px #888;
}

/* Example 2: Shadow with negative offsets for a top-left
effect */
.box {
    box-shadow: -3px -3px 5px #888;
}
```

In Example 1, we create a simple shadow with a horizontal offset of 3 pixels, a vertical offset of 3 pixels, a blur radius of 5 pixels, and a color of #888 (a gray color). The result is a subtle shadow that gives the element a sense of elevation.

In Example 2, we use negative offsets to create a top-left shadow effect. The element appears as if it is floating above the surface, with the shadow indicating that it is lifted off the page.

Multiple Shadows for Complex Effects

The real power of the box-shadow property lies in its ability to handle multiple shadows, allowing us to achieve more complex and visually stunning effects. Let's look at an example of how we can combine multiple shadows.

Here is the CSS:

```
/* Example 3: Multiple shadows for a deep 3D effect */
.box {
    box-shadow:
        0 0 5px rgba(0, 0, 0, 0.2), /* Light gray shadow */
        0 6px 10px -5px rgba(0, 0, 0, 0.4), /* Dark gray shadow
        with blur */
        0 10px 20px rgba(0, 0, 0, 0.1); /* Lighter shadow at the
        bottom */
}
```

In the previous code, we use three shadows to create a deep 3D effect. The first shadow is a subtle, light gray shadow with no blur. The second shadow is a dark gray shadow with a blur radius of 10 pixels, offset vertically by 6 pixels and slightly moved up by 5 pixels (negative spread distance). This creates the illusion of a shadow cast by a raised element.

Finally, the third shadow is a lighter, soft shadow at the bottom of the element, giving it a grounded appearance. The combination of these shadows adds depth and dimension to the element, making it stand out from the page.

Inset Shadows: Creating Sunken Elements

Another interesting use of the box-shadow property is to create inset shadows, which can make elements appear sunken into the page.

Here is the CSS:

```
/* Example 4: Inset shadow for a sunken effect */
.box {
    box-shadow: inset 0 0 5px rgba(0, 0, 0, 0.2);
}
```

In the previous code, we use an inset shadow with no offsets (0 0) and a blur radius of 5 pixels. The inset keyword tells the browser to apply the shadow inside the element instead of outside. This creates a sunken effect, making the element look like it is pressed into the surface.

Creating Text Shadows

The box-shadow property is not limited to box elements; it can also be used to add shadows to text. Text shadows can be particularly useful for creating eye-catching headings and other prominent text elements.

Here is the CSS:

```css
/* Example 5: Text shadow for an eye-catching heading */
h1 {
    font-size: 36px;
    color: #333;
    text-shadow: 2px 2px 4px rgba(0, 0, 0, 0.2);
}
```

In the previous code, we apply a text shadow to an h1 element with a horizontal offset of 2 pixels, a vertical offset of 2 pixels, a blur radius of 4 pixels, and a color that is a semi-transparent black. This shadow enhances the visibility of the heading, making it pop out from the background.

The box-shadow property in CSS3 is a powerful tool that allows designers to add depth, dimension, and creative effects to their web designs. By understanding how to use horizontal and vertical offsets, blur radii, spread distances, and colors, you can create a wide range of shadow effects to suit your design needs. Whether you want to add subtle shadows for elevation or create complex 3D effects, the box-shadow property empowers you to craft visually stunning and engaging web interfaces.

Remember to experiment and combine multiple shadows to unlock the full potential of this CSS3 feature. With box-shadow, you can bring your web designs to life and captivate your audience with captivating visual experiences. So, go ahead, dive into the world of shadows, and elevate your design game!

Background Gradients

In CSS3, you can create background gradients using the background-image property with the linear-gradient() or radial-gradient() functions. Gradients allow you to smoothly blend multiple colors together, creating visually appealing and dynamic backgrounds for your web elements. Let's explore how to use these functions to create linear and radial gradients.

- **Linear gradient**

  A linear gradient creates a smooth transition between two or more colors along a straight line. The linear-gradient() function takes a direction parameter, which defines the angle or direction of the gradient. Let's look at a basic example.

  Here is the CSS:

  ```
  /* Example 1: Creating a vertical linear gradient */
  .element {
      width: 300px;
      height: 200px;
      background-image: linear-gradient(to bottom,
  #f00, #00f);
  }
  ```

In this example, the .element will have a background that starts with a red color (#f00) at the top and transitions to blue (#00f) at the bottom. The to bottom parameter specifies that the gradient should be from the top to the bottom. You can use other directions like to top, to left, to right, or specific angles like 45deg or 135deg to control the direction of the gradient.

- **Radial gradient**

  A radial gradient creates a smooth transition between colors radiating from a center point. The radial-gradient() function allows you to define the shape and size of the gradient. Let's look at an example.

  Here is the CSS:

```
/* Example 2: Creating a radial gradient */
.element {
    width: 200px;
    height: 200px;
    background-image: radial-gradient(circle,
#ff0, #0f0);
}
```

  In this example, the .element will have a background that starts with a yellow color (#ff0) at the center and transitions to green (#0f0) toward the edges. The circle parameter indicates that the gradient should be a perfect circle. You can use other shapes like ellipse or define specific sizes like at 50% 50% to control the center point of the gradient.

- **Multiple color stops**

  Gradients can contain multiple color stops, allowing
  for more complex and customized backgrounds.
  Color stops define where the transition between
  colors occurs. You can add as many color stops as
  needed. Let's look at an example.

  Here is the CSS:

  ```css
  /* Example 3: Linear gradient with multiple color
  stops */
  .element {
      width: 400px;
      height: 200px;
      background-image: linear-gradient(to right, #f00,
      #ff0, #0f0);
  }
  ```

  In this example, the .element will have a background
  with three color stops: red (#f00) on the left,
  transitioning to yellow (#ff0) in the middle, and finally
  to green (#0f0) on the right.

- **Using color stops with percentage or specific lengths**

  You can control the position of each color stop using
  percentages or specific lengths. This allows you to
  fine-tune the gradient's appearance. Let's look at an
  example.

  Here is the CSS:

  ```css
  /* Example 4: Radial gradient with specific color stop
  positions */
  .element {
  ```

```
    width: 200px;
    height: 200px;
    background-image: radial-gradient(circle at 60%
    40%, #f00 10%, #0f0 70%);
}
```

In this example, the .element will have a radial gradient that starts with red (#f00) at 10 percent from the center and transitions to green (#0f0) at 70 percent from the center. The center of the gradient is positioned at 60 percent of the container's width and 40 percent of the container's height.

- **Using multiple gradients**

  You can also layer multiple gradients on top of each other to create more complex effects. Let's look at an example.

  Here is the CSS:

```
/* Example 5: Multiple gradients layered together */
.element {
    width: 300px;
    height: 200px;
    background-image:
      linear-gradient(to right, #f00, #ff0),
      radial-gradient(circle, #0f0, #00f);
}
```

In this example, the .element will have a linear gradient from red (#f00) to yellow (#ff0) on the left side and a radial gradient from green (#0f0) to blue (#00f) on the right side. The gradients are layered on top of each other, creating a unique and visually interesting background.

With CSS3 background gradients, you can unleash your creativity and design stunning backgrounds for your web elements. Experiment with different colors, directions, shapes, and color stops to achieve the desired effects and enhance the overall aesthetics of your web design. Gradients are a powerful tool that can help you create visually engaging and modern interfaces that captivate your users.

Repeating Gradients

In CSS3, you can create repeating gradients using the repeating-linear-gradient() and repeating-radial-gradient() functions. Repeating gradients allow you to create a seamless pattern by repeating the gradient at regular intervals. This can be particularly useful for creating backgrounds and textures. Let's explore how to use these functions to create repeating gradients.

- **Repeating linear gradient**

  The repeating-linear-gradient() function allows you to create a repeating linear gradient. It works similarly to the linear-gradient() function, but with an additional parameter that defines the size of the repeating pattern. Let's look at an example.

  Here is the CSS:

```
/* Example 1: Creating a repeating linear gradient */
.element {
    width: 400px;
    height: 100px;
    background-image: repeating-linear-gradient(to
    right, #f00, #ff0 30px, #0f0 30px, #0f0 60px);
}
```

In this example, the .element will have a repeating linear gradient that starts with red (#f00) on the left and transitions to yellow (#ff0) at 30 pixels, then transitions to green (#0f0) at 30 pixels, and finally repeats the pattern. The repeating pattern will continue horizontally to the right.

- **Repeating radial gradient**

The repeating-radial-gradient() function allows you to create a repeating radial gradient. It works similarly to the radial-gradient() function, but with an additional parameter that defines the size of the repeating pattern. Let's look at an example.

Here is the CSS:

```
/* Example 2: Creating a repeating radial gradient */
.element {
    width: 200px;
    height: 200px;
    background-image: repeating-radial-gradient(circle,
    #f00, #0f0 20px);
}
```

In this example, the .element will have a repeating radial gradient that starts with red (#f00) at the center and transitions to green (#0f0) at 20 pixels from the center. The repeating pattern will continue radially outward from the center.

- **Repeating multiple gradients**

  You can also create more complex repeating
  gradients by layering multiple gradients together.
  This allows you to create intricate patterns and
  textures. Let's look at an example.

  Here is the CSS:

```
/* Example 3: Repeating multiple gradients */
.element {
    width: 300px;
    height: 300px;
    background-image:
        repeating-linear-gradient(to right, #f00, #ff0
        20px, #0f0 20px, #0f0 40px),
        repeating-radial-gradient(circle, #00f,
        #0f0 20px);
}
```

  In this example, the .element will have a repeating
  linear gradient that starts with red (#f00) on the
  left, transitions to yellow (#ff0) at 20 pixels, then
  transitions to green (#0f0) at 20 pixels, and finally
  repeats the pattern horizontally. Additionally, the
  element will also have a repeating radial gradient
  that starts with blue (#00f) at the center and
  transitions to green (#0f0) at 20 pixels from the
  center. Both gradients are layered together, creating
  a visually engaging repeating pattern.

Repeating gradients in CSS3 offer a powerful way to create seamless
and visually appealing backgrounds and textures for your web elements.
By experimenting with different colors, directions, shapes, and pattern

sizes, you can achieve unique and eye-catching designs that add depth and interest to your web pages. So, go ahead and unleash your creativity with repeating gradients to enhance the aesthetics of your web design!

Multiple Background Images

In CSS3, you can apply multiple background images to an element using the background-image property. Each background image is separated by a comma within the background-image property value. This allows you to layer multiple images on an element, creating various visual effects. Let's explore how to use multiple background images in CSS3.

- **Applying multiple background images**

  Here is the CSS:

  ```
  /* Example 1: Applying multiple background images */
  .element {
      width: 300px;
      height: 200px;
      background-image:
        url('image1.jpg'),
        url('image2.jpg');
  }
  ```

  In this example, the .element will have two background images layered on top of each other. The first image is image1.jpg, and the second image is image2.jpg. By default, the images are layered from front to back, meaning that the first image is at the top, and subsequent images are underneath. See Figure 7-5.

Figure 7-5. *Multiple images layered on each other at 50 percent size*

- **Positioning and sizing background images**

  You can control the positioning and sizing of each background image by providing additional parameters like background-position and background-size. Let's look at an example.

  Here is the CSS:

```css
/* Example 2: Positioning and sizing multiple
background images */
.element {
    width: 300px;
    height: 200px;
    background-image:
      url('image1.jpg'),
      url('image2.jpg');
    background-position: top left, center;
    background-size: cover, 50%;
}
```

  In this example, the first background image image1.jpg is positioned at the top-left corner of the .element, and its size is set to cover the entire element. The second background image, image2.

jpg, is centered and sized to cover 50 percent of the element's width and height. This code would produce the same output as shown in Figure 7-5.

- **Controlling background image layering**

  You can control the layering order of the background images using the background shorthand property or the background-layer property. By adjusting the order of the background images, you can achieve different visual effects. Let's look at an example.

  Here is the CSS:

```css
/* Example 3: Controlling background image layering */
.element {
    width: 300px;
    height: 200px;
    background-image:
      url('image1.jpg'),
      url('image2.jpg');
    background-position: top left, center;
    background-size: cover, 50%;
    background-layer: 2, 1;
}
```

In this example, the background-layer property is used to specify the layering order of the background images. The image2.jpg image is positioned at the top layer (layer 1), while image1.jpg is placed behind it (layer 2). By reversing the order, you can achieve a different layering effect.

- **Repeating multiple background images**

  You can also apply repeating background images using the repeating-linear-gradient() and repeating-radial-gradient() functions, as demonstrated in the previous responses about repeating gradients.

With multiple background images in CSS3, you have a powerful tool to create intricate and visually engaging backgrounds for your web elements. By experimenting with different images, positions, sizes, and layering orders, you can achieve unique and eye-catching designs that enhance the aesthetics and user experience of your web pages.

Sizable Icons for Responsive Design

When it comes to creating sizeable icons perfect for responsive design, scalable vector icons are the ideal choice. Scalable vector icons are graphics represented as vector shapes rather than pixel-based images, which means they can be easily resized without losing quality or becoming pixelated. Here are some popular formats for scalable vector icons that work well for responsive design:

- *Scalable Vector Graphics (SVG)*: SVG is the most widely used format for scalable vector icons in web development. It is an XML-based format that defines vector shapes using mathematical equations. SVG icons can be easily resized using CSS or attributes without any loss of quality. They are well-supported by all modern browsers, making them a perfect choice for responsive design.

- *Icon fonts*: Icon fonts are another popular way to create scalable icons. They use font glyphs to represent icons, and you can easily adjust their size with CSS just like regular text. Icon fonts are widely supported and can be used in responsive designs with relative ease. However, they might not be the most accessible option for screen readers and may have some limitations compared to SVG.

- *CSS shapes and backgrounds*: With CSS, you can create scalable icons using CSS shapes and backgrounds. This involves using CSS properties such as border-radius and background-image to create vector-based shapes. This method is suitable for simple geometric icons and can be resized responsively using media queries or percentage-based dimensions.

- *Icon libraries and frameworks*: There are numerous icon libraries and frameworks available that provide a wide variety of predesigned scalable icons. Some popular ones include Font Awesome, Material Icons, and Ionicons. These icon libraries are usually available in SVG format and come with CSS classes for easy integration into responsive designs.

Best Practices for Using Scalable Icons in Responsive Design

Here are some best practices:

- *Use SVG whenever possible*: SVG is the most versatile and widely supported format for scalable icons. It provides excellent quality at any size and is the best choice for responsive designs.

197

- *Optimize SVG files*: SVG files can sometimes contain unnecessary elements or attributes, making them larger than necessary. Use SVG optimization tools to reduce file size and improve loading times.

- *Use icon font subsetting*: If you choose to use icon fonts, consider using subsetting techniques to include only the icons you need. This reduces the font file size and improves performance.

- *Use relative sizing*: When using CSS to size icons, prefer relative units such as percentages or ems over fixed pixel values. This ensures that icons scale proportionally with their containers.

- *Test across devices and resolutions*: Always test your responsive designs across various devices and resolutions to ensure that the icons look good and retain their quality at different screen sizes.

- *Consider accessibility*: Ensure that your icons are accessible to all users, including those with screen readers. Provide alternative text or ARIA attributes for icon elements.

By following these best practices and choosing scalable vector icon formats, you can create perfect icons for responsive design that adapt seamlessly to different screen sizes and resolutions.

Summary

This chapter covered various techniques to add shadow effects. The first and simplest way is to add shadows to text. Knowing what color values are allowed is important as is knowing how to prevent text shadows. Adding an embossed effect to text shadow the right way enhances the UX experience. It is not restricted to only one shadow effect; multiple effects can be added. The chapter also covered box shadows and background gradients, both linear and radial. We also covered icons and best practices.

CHAPTER 8

Forms with HTML

HTML forms are an integral part of creating any website that requires user input. The form element binds this data and sends it to the server side to be stored in data storage. This chapter covers various form elements and explains how to create an HTML5 form. It also discusses all these form elements in detail with code examples for better understanding of real-world use cases. This chapter explains how to handle errors and validations using HTML5 forms. This chapter covers accessibility options along with how these forms work on mobile devices and covers the new elements introduced in HTML5 in detail. Finally, the chapter covers how to support older versions of browsers by using a polyfill.

HTML5 Forms

HTML5, the latest version of the Hypertext Markup Language, introduced significant improvements to web forms, revolutionizing the way we collect user data and enhancing the overall user experience. In this section, we will delve into the world of HTML5 forms, exploring their new features, benefits, and best practices for creating powerful and user-friendly web forms.

© Varun Gor 2023
V. Gor, *Creating Responsive Websites Using HTML5 and CSS3*,
https://doi.org/10.1007/978-1-4842-9783-4_8

- **Semantic form elements**

  HTML5 introduced several semantic form elements that provide more meaning and context to form fields. These elements include <input type="email">, <input type="url">, <input type="tel">, and <input type="date">, among others. By using these elements, you can validate user input and guide users to enter the correct format of data. For example, the <input type="email"> element ensures that users enter a valid email address, while <input type="date"> presents users with a date picker for easy date selection.

- **Input types and attributes**

  HTML5 brought a wealth of new input types and attributes to customize form fields according to specific data requirements. Some of the input types include color picker (<input type="color">), range slider (<input type="range">), and number input with min and max values (<input type="number" min="0" max="100">). Additionally, the required attribute allows you to mark certain fields as mandatory, preventing form submission until they are filled.

- **Placeholder and autofocus**

  The placeholder attribute allows you to provide hints or example values within form fields, guiding users on the expected input. For example, <input type="text" placeholder="Enter your name"> displays "Enter your name" inside the input field. Additionally, the autofocus attribute automatically sets the focus on a specific form field when the page loads, making it more convenient for users to start entering data without the need for manual clicks.

- **Validation and error handling**

  HTML5 introduced built-in form validation, reducing the reliance on JavaScript for basic data validation. Using attributes such as pattern, min, max, and step, you can define acceptable formats and value ranges for input fields. For example, <input type="number" min="1" max="10" step="1"> ensures that users enter a number between 1 and 10. In the case of invalid input, browsers display appropriate error messages, enhancing the user experience.

- **New form elements**

  HTML5 introduced several new form elements that were previously accomplished using custom scripts or plugins. The <datalist> element allows you to provide a predefined list of options for an input field, making it easier for users to select from available choices. Additionally, the <textarea> element now supports the maxlength attribute, which allows you to limit the number of characters a user can input.

- **Accessibility considerations**

  When designing HTML5 forms, it is essential to consider accessibility to ensure that all users, including those with disabilities, can interact with the form effectively. Using proper labeling with <label> elements and associating them with form fields using the for attribute or by nesting them inside the respective field helps screen readers and other assistive technologies understand the form's structure.

- **Mobile and responsive forms**

  With the rise of mobile usage, creating responsive forms that adapt to various screen sizes and orientations is crucial. HTML5 forms provide a solid foundation for building mobile-friendly forms. When designing for mobile, consider using the appropriate input types and optimizing the form layout for smaller screens to enhance the mobile user experience.

HTML5 forms have transformed the way we collect user data on the Web. With new semantic elements, input types, attributes, and built-in validation, web developers can create powerful and user-friendly forms that improve data accuracy and enhance the overall user experience. By leveraging the capabilities of HTML5 forms and considering accessibility and responsiveness, web designers can ensure that their forms are efficient, accessible, and appealing to users across all devices and platforms. Embracing HTML5 forms is an essential step toward creating modern, dynamic, and user-centric web applications.

Figure 8-1 shows a simple user registration form without any CSS.

Figure 8-1. *HTML displaying form elements in Chrome*

Decoding the HTML5 Form Elements

HTML5 forms can be really heavy handling all the fields with so much of the information to be put in. Let's cover the HTML code provided earlier. The form consists of an ID and method (get or post).

```
<form id-"user_registration" method="post">
```

The form elements have three sections: a fieldset, a legend, and each input element wrapped around a <div> (which can be observed in the following code):

```
<fieldset>
        <legend>Personal Information:</legend>
        <div>
            <label for="name">Name:</label>
            <input type="text" id="u_name" name="u_
            name" required aria-required="true"
            placeholder="John Doe">

        </div>
        <div>
            <label for="email">Email Address:</label>
            <input type="text" id="u_email" name="u_email"
            required aria-required="true" placeholder="John.
            Doe@example.com">
        </div>
        <div>
            <label for="phone">Phone Number:</label>
            <input type="text" id="u_phone" name="u_
            phone" required aria-required="true"
            placeholder="987-654-321">
        </div>
        <div>
```

```
        <label for="linkedin">LinkedIn Profile:</label>
        <input type="text" id="u_linkedin" name="u_
        linkedin " required aria-required="true"
        placeholder="https://www.linkedin.com/in/johndoe/">
    </div>
</fieldset>
```

Input Type

The input type denotes the type of input and various validations along with whether the field is mandatory or not. Examples of input types are text box, text area, checkbox, drop-downs, radio buttons, etc. The input type element most commonly has id and name attributes, and its validation can be controlled by JavaScript or mentioning specific tags like required or aria-required. It also can have a placeholder value that can be used to direct a user to indicate what values the input field will be accepting.

required

A Boolean value is used to indicate if the input field is mandatory for the user to provide a value. The following values can be used to do so:

required aria-required="true"

required is a Boolean value, and if mentioned with the input field, it will make that field mandatory, whereas aria-required will take true or false as a value and marks the field mandatory only if its value is marked true. If the form is submitted without the field containing the required value(s) or containing incorrect values, an error message is displayed that is specific to this particular field and to the browser.

placeholder

This is how placeholder code can be written:

placeholder="e.g. 987-654-3210"

The placeholder value is displayed by default in the field where this is defined. The previous example denotes a phone number and will be displayed by default. The user can click the input field and provide the phone number, and the field value will now contain the user-provided input. If this field is in focus and the user has yet to enter the value, the placeholder value disappears, and it will magically come back if the focus is moved from this particular input field and the user has not entered any value for it.

autofocus

The autofocus attribute is a Boolean attribute that can be applied to certain form elements to automatically set the focus on them when the page loads. When an element has the autofocus attribute, it becomes the active element on the page, which means the user can start interacting with it immediately without needing to manually click or tap the field.

The autofocus attribute can be used with a variety of form elements, such as text inputs, text areas, checkboxes, radio buttons, and buttons. However, it's essential to use it judiciously to avoid overwhelming users with unnecessary focus changes, which could disrupt their browsing experience.

Points to Consider

Consider the following points:

- *Only one autofocus element*: It's essential to use the autofocus attribute sparingly and on only one form element per page. If you use it on multiple elements, the last one in the HTML document will receive focus. Having multiple autofocus elements can lead to a confusing and jarring user experience.

- *Impact on accessibility*: While using autofocus can be convenient for users, it's essential to consider accessibility. When a form field is automatically focused, users who rely on screen readers or other assistive technologies might not be aware of the change. Make sure to provide clear labels and instructions for autofocus fields to ensure that all users understand the context.

- *Focus order*: The autofocus attribute affects the initial focus when the page loads. After the user interacts with the form and presses the Tab key to move between fields, the focus order follows the natural tabbing order of the form elements, unless otherwise specified using other attributes like tabindex.

- *HTML5 support*: The autofocus attribute is supported in all modern web browsers. However, for compatibility with older browsers, consider providing fallback behavior through JavaScript, which can programmatically set focus on the desired element.

autocomplete

The autocomplete attribute is used to control whether a web browser should remember the autofill form field values based on the user's previous input. The attribute is applied to individual form fields to specify whether the browser should provide suggestions for that particular field. The autocomplete attribute can be set to different values to control the autofill behavior.

The autocomplete attribute can be applied to various types of form fields, such as text inputs, passwords, email addresses, and more. It is particularly useful for login forms, registration forms, and other types of forms where users often enter the same information repeatedly.

Usage of autocomplete Attribute

Here's how to use the autocomplete attributes:

- **On/off (Boolean value)**

  - *autocomplete="on"*: The default behavior. The browser is allowed to remember and suggest previously entered values for the field.

  - *autocomplete="off"*: The browser should not remember or suggest previously entered values for the field.

- **Using specific values (string value)**

  The autocomplete attribute can also take specific string values that allow developers to fine-tune autofill behavior based on the type of data being entered:

  - *autocomplete="name"*: Suggests previously entered names, like usernames, first names, or last names

  - *autocomplete="email"*: Suggests previously entered email addresses

209

- *autocomplete="password"*: Prevents the browser from suggesting previously entered passwords, providing an additional layer of security

- *autocomplete="current-password"*: Suggests previously entered passwords that are used for the current site or application

- *autocomplete="new-password"*: Suggests previously entered passwords for creating a new account or changing the password

- *autocomplete="address-line1" and autocomplete="address-line2"*: Suggests parts of the user's address for forms that collect address information

- *autocomplete="country"*: Suggests previously entered countries

- *autocomplete="postal-code"*: Suggests previously entered postal codes

- *autocomplete="tel"*: Suggests previously entered telephone numbers

- *autocomplete="credit-card-name"*: Suggests previously entered credit card holder names

- *autocomplete="credit-card-number"*: Suggests previously entered credit card numbers

- *autocomplete="credit-card-expiry"*: Suggests previously entered credit card expiry dates

- *autocomplete="credit-card-cvc"*: Suggests previously entered credit card verification codes

Note   While the autocomplete attribute provides control over autofill behavior, modern browsers have their own algorithms for deciding when and how to use this information. Additionally, some browsers might ignore the autocomplete attribute for sensitive information, such as passwords, to protect user privacy and security.

By leveraging the autocomplete attribute appropriately, you can provide a more streamlined and user-friendly experience for users, especially for forms where they frequently enter similar information. However, it's essential to use it thoughtfully and consider user privacy and security concerns while implementing autofill features in your web forms.

dropdown and Its Associated Values

The <list> and <datalist> elements work together to create predefined lists of options for an input field. The <datalist> element provides a set of predefined options that users can choose from, while the <input> element with the list attribute associates itself with the <datalist> element and displays the options as suggestions when the user interacts with the input field.

The <datalist> Element

The <datalist> element is used to define a set of predefined options that can be associated with an input field. It contains a list of <option> elements, each representing an option in the list. The user can select one of these options from the drop-down list when they interact with the associated input field.

```
<!DOCTYPE html>
<html>
<head>
  <title>Datalist Example</title>
</head>
<body>
  <label for="programmingLanguage">Select a programming
  language:</label>
  <input type="text" id="programmingLanguage" list="languages">

  <datalist id="languages">
    <option value="JavaScript">
    <option value="Python">
    <option value="Java">
    <option value="C++">
    <option value="Ruby">
  </datalist>
</body>
</html>
```

In this example, we have an input field with the ID
programmingLanguage and a <datalist> element with the ID languages.
The <datalist> contains several <option> elements, each with a value
attribute representing different programming languages. When the user
interacts with the input field, the browser displays a drop-down list of the
available programming languages as suggestions.

The <input> Element with the list Attribute

To associate an input field with a <datalist>, you use the list attribute on
the <input> element and set it to the ID of the corresponding <datalist>.
This association enables the browser to display the predefined options as
suggestions when the user interacts with the input field.

```
<!DOCTYPE html>
<html>
<head>
  <title>Datalist Example</title>
</head>
<body>
  <label for="programmingLanguage">Select a programming
  language:</label>
  <input type="text" id="programmingLanguage" list="languages">

  <datalist id="languages">
    <option value="JavaScript">
    <option value="Python">
    <option value="Java">
    <option value="C++">
    <option value="Ruby">
  </datalist>
</body>
</html>
```

In this example, the <input> element with the ID programmingLanguage has the list attribute set to languages, which corresponds to the ID of the <datalist>. As a result, when the user interacts with the input field, the browser displays the predefined programming languages from the <datalist> as suggestions. See Figure 8-2 and Figure 8-3.

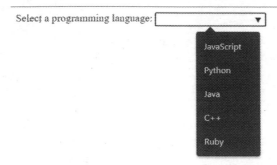

Figure 8-2. *HTML displaying <datalist> elements in Chrome*

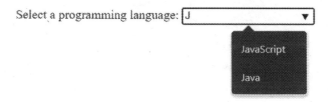

Figure 8-3. *HTML displaying <datalist> elements in Chrome when user types in a character*

Note

- The <datalist> element is not visible on the page. It acts as a behind-the-scenes data source for the associated input field.

- The options defined in the <datalist> are suggestions, but the user can still type a custom value in the input field if they don't want to choose from the predefined options.

- The <datalist> element is supported by most modern
  web browsers, but older browsers might not support
  it. However, the input field will still work as a regular
  text input without the drop-down suggestions in
  unsupported browsers.

HTML5 Input Types

HTML5 introduced various input types that enhance the functionality and
user experience of web forms. These input types allow developers to create
more specialized and user-friendly input fields, tailored to specific data
types. Let's explore the most commonly used HTML5 input types:

- *Text input (type="text")*: The default input type for
  single-line text. It's suitable for general text input, such
  as names, emails, and short messages.

- *Password input (type="password")*: This conceals
  the entered text, typically used for password fields to
  protect sensitive information.

- *Number input (type="number")*: This allows users to
  enter numeric values. You can use the min, max, and
  step attributes to set limits and define the numeric
  increment.

- *Email input (type="email")*: This is optimized for
  entering email addresses. It can trigger email-specific
  validation, such as checking for a valid email format.

- *URL input (type="url")*: This is intended for entering
  URLs (web addresses). It can trigger URL-specific
  validation, such as ensuring a valid URL format.

- *Tel input (type="tel")*: This is designed for entering telephone numbers. It can be useful for mobile devices as it may display a numeric keypad.

- *Date input (type="date")*: This provides a date picker to facilitate selecting a date. The format displayed might vary between browsers.

- *Time input (type="time")*: This offers a time picker for selecting a specific time, such as hours and minutes.

- *Datetime input (type="datetime-local")*: This combines date and time input, allowing users to choose a specific date and time.

- *Month input (type="month")*: This enables users to select a month and year, useful for selecting month/year combinations.

- *Week input (type="week")*: This allows users to choose a week and year, useful for selecting a week in the calendar.

- *Color input (type="color")*: This presents a color picker to choose a color value.

- *Checkbox input (type="checkbox")*: This represents a checkbox, allowing users to select one or more options.

- *Radio input (type="radio")*: This represents a radio button, allowing users to choose one option from a group of mutually exclusive options.

- *File input (type="file")*: This creates a file upload button, enabling users to upload files from their local devices.

- *Search input (type="search")*: This provides styling cues for a search input field and, in some cases, might trigger specific search behaviors.

- *Range input (type="range")*: This displays a slider to choose a value within a specified range, useful for numeric inputs like volume controls.

- *Submit input (type="submit")*: This represents a submit button in a form, which submits the form data to the server.

- *Reset input (type="reset")*: This represents a reset button, which resets the form fields to their default values.

- *Button input (type="button")*: This represents a generic button, often used to trigger custom JavaScript functions.

These HTML5 input types enrich web forms by providing specialized input controls and validation for specific data types. By utilizing the appropriate input types, developers can create more intuitive and efficient user interfaces, leading to a better user experience and improved data accuracy.

Text Input

The input element with type="text" is used to create a single-line text input field in web forms. This input type is one of the most commonly used and allows users to enter plain text, such as names, email addresses, messages, or any other free-form textual information.

Here's the basic syntax of the text input:

```
<input type="text" name="inputName" id="inputID" value="Initial
text" placeholder="Enter your text here">
```

Let's explore the attributes and characteristics of the text input:

- *type="text"*: This attribute specifies the type of the input element, which, in this case, is text.

- *name*: The name attribute is used to define a name for the input element. It is essential for form submission, as it identifies the input field and its associated value in the form data.

- *id*: The id attribute provides a unique identifier for the input element, allowing you to associate labels with the input using the for attribute.

- *value*: The value attribute sets the initial value of the input field. Users can edit this value, and it will be submitted along with the form data.

- *placeholder*: The placeholder attribute is used to display a short hint or example text inside the input field when it is empty. It provides guidance to users on what type of information to enter.

- *size*: The size attribute determines the visible width of the input field in terms of characters. It does not restrict the number of characters a user can input; it affects only the visual display.

- *maxlength*: The maxlength attribute defines the maximum number of characters that a user can input into the text field.

- *autofocus*: The autofocus attribute, when present, automatically sets the focus on the text input when the page loads, allowing users to start typing without manually selecting the field.

Password Input

The input element with type="password" is used to create a password input field in web forms. This input type is specifically designed for entering sensitive information, such as passwords or other confidential data, and it masks the characters entered by the user to protect their privacy.

Here's the basic syntax of the password input:

```
<input type="password" name="passwordField"
id="passwordFieldID" placeholder="Enter your password">
```

Let's explore the attributes and characteristics of the password input:

- *type="password"*: This attribute specifies the type of the input element, which, in this case, is password.

- *name*: The name attribute is used to define a name for the input element. It is essential for form submission, as it identifies the input field and its associated value in the form data.

- *id*: The id attribute provides a unique identifier for the input element, allowing you to associate labels with the input using the for attribute.

- *placeholder*: The placeholder attribute is used to display a short hint inside the input field when it is empty. It provides a prompt to users to enter their password without revealing the actual characters.

- *size*: The size attribute determines the visible width of the input field in terms of characters. It does not restrict the number of characters a user can input; it affects only the visual display.

- *maxlength*: The maxlength attribute defines the maximum number of characters that a user can input into the password field.

- *autofocus*: The autofocus attribute, when present, automatically sets the focus on the password input when the page loads, making it convenient for users to start typing their password.

Number Input

The input element with type="number" is used to create a numeric input field in web forms. This input type is specifically designed for accepting numeric values, such as integers or floating-point numbers. The number input provides additional controls such as arrows to increase or decrease the numeric value, making it easier for users to input numeric data.

Here's the basic syntax of the number input:

```
<input type="number" name="numberField" id="numberFieldID"
min="minValue" max="maxValue" step="stepValue">
```

Let's explore the attributes and characteristics of the number input:

- *type="number"*: This attribute specifies the type of the input element, which, in this case, is number.

- *name*: The name attribute is used to define a name for the input element. It is essential for form submission, as it identifies the input field and its associated value in the form data.

- *id*: The id attribute provides a unique identifier for the input element, allowing you to associate labels with the input using the for attribute.

- *min*: The min attribute sets the minimum value that the input field can accept. Users cannot enter a value lower than the specified minimum.

- *max*: The max attribute sets the maximum value that the input field can accept. Users cannot enter a value higher than the specified maximum.

- *step*: The step attribute defines the increment or decrement step for the numeric value. For example, if step="0.5", users can enter values only in increments of 0.5.

- *value*: The value attribute sets the initial value of the input field. Users can edit this value, and it will be submitted along with the form data.

- *size*: The size attribute determines the visible width of the input field in terms of characters. It does not restrict the number of characters a user can input; it affects only the visual display.

Email Input

The input element with type="email" is used to create an email input field in web forms. This input type is specifically designed for collecting email addresses from users and provides built-in email validation to ensure that the entered value is in a valid email format.

Here's the basic syntax of the email input:

```
<input type="email" name="emailField" id="emailFieldID"
placeholder="Enter your email">
```

Let's explore the attributes and characteristics of the email input:

- *type="email"*: This attribute specifies the type of the input element, which, in this case, is "email."

- *name*: The name attribute is used to define a name for the input element. It is essential for form submission, as it identifies the input field and its associated value in the form data.

- *id*: The id attribute provides a unique identifier for the input element, allowing you to associate labels with the input using the for attribute.

- *placeholder*: The placeholder attribute is used to display a short hint inside the input field when it is empty. It provides guidance to users on what type of information to enter, such as "Enter your email."

- *value*: The value attribute sets the initial value of the input field. Users can edit this value, and it will be submitted along with the form data.

- *required*: The required attribute, when present, makes the email input a required field, meaning that users must fill it out before submitting the form.

URL Input

The input element with type="url" is used to create a URL input field in web forms. This input type is specifically designed for collecting web addresses (URLs) from users and provides built-in URL validation to ensure that the entered value is in a valid URL format.

Here's the basic syntax of the URL input:

```
<input type="url" name="urlField" id="urlFieldID"
placeholder="Enter a URL">
```

Let's explore the attributes and characteristics of the URL input:

- *type="url"*: This attribute specifies the type of the input element, which, in this case, is "url."

- *name*: The name attribute is used to define a name for the input element. It is essential for form submission, as it identifies the input field and its associated value in the form data.

- *id*: The id attribute provides a unique identifier for the input element, allowing you to associate labels with the input using the for attribute.

- *placeholder*: The placeholder attribute is used to display a short hint inside the input field when it is empty. It provides guidance to users on what type of information to enter, such as "Enter a URL."

- *value*: The value attribute sets the initial value of the input field. Users can edit this value, and it will be submitted along with the form data.

- *required*: The required attribute, when present, makes the URL input a required field, meaning that users must fill it out before submitting the form.

Tel Input

The input element with type="tel" is used to create a telephone number input field in web forms. This input type is specifically designed for collecting telephone numbers from users and provides features that are beneficial for mobile devices, such as displaying a numeric keypad when focused.

Here's the basic syntax of the telephone number input:

```
<input type="tel" name="phoneField" id="phoneFieldID"
placeholder="Enter your phone number">
```

Let's explore the attributes and characteristics of the telephone number input:

- *type="tel"*: This attribute specifies the type of the input element, which, in this case, is tel.

- *name*: The name attribute is used to define a name for the input element. It is essential for form submission, as it identifies the input field and its associated value in the form data.

- *id*: The id attribute provides a unique identifier for the input element, allowing you to associate labels with the input using the for attribute.

- *placeholder*: The placeholder attribute is used to display a short hint inside the input field when it is empty. It provides guidance to users on what type of information to enter, such as "Enter your phone number."

- *value*: The value attribute sets the initial value of the input field. Users can edit this value, and it will be submitted along with the form data.

- *required*: The required attribute, when present, makes the telephone number input a required field, meaning that users must fill it out before submitting the form.

Date Input

The input element with type="date" is used to create a date input field in web forms. This input type is specifically designed for collecting dates from users and provides a date picker or calendar widget, making it easier for users to select a date.

Here's the basic syntax of the date input:

```
<input type="date" name="dateField" id="dateFieldID">
```

Let's explore the attributes and characteristics of the date input:

- *type="date"*: This attribute specifies the type of the input element, which, in this case, is date.

- *name*: The name attribute is used to define a name for the input element. It is essential for form submission, as it identifies the input field and its associated value in the form data.

- *id*: The id attribute provides a unique identifier for the input element, allowing you to associate labels with the input using the for attribute.

- *value*: The value attribute sets the initial value of the input field. It should be in the format "YYYY-MM-DD," representing the date in year-month-day order.

- *min*: The min attribute sets the minimum date that the input field can accept. Users cannot select a date earlier than the specified minimum.

- *max*: The max attribute sets the maximum date that the input field can accept. Users cannot select a date later than the specified maximum.

- *step*: The step attribute defines the increment or decrement step for the date input. It controls the granularity of the available date options. For example, step="1" represents one day, step="2" represents two days, and so on.

- *required*: The required attribute, when present, makes the date input a required field, meaning that users must select a date before submitting the form.

Time Input

The input element with type="time" is used to create a time input field in web forms. This input type is specifically designed for collecting time values from users and provides a time picker, making it easier for users to select a specific time.

Here's the basic syntax of the time input:

```
<input type="time" name="timeField" id="timeFieldID">
```

Let's explore the attributes and characteristics of the time input:

- *type="time"*: This attribute specifies the type of the input element, which, in this case, is time.

- *name*: The name attribute is used to define a name for the input element. It is essential for form submission, as it identifies the input field and its associated value in the form data.

- *id*: The id attribute provides a unique identifier for the input element, allowing you to associate labels with the input using the for attribute.

- *value*: The value attribute sets the initial value of the input field. It should be in the format HH:mm, representing the time in hours and minutes.

- *min*: The min attribute sets the minimum time that the input field can accept. Users cannot select a time earlier than the specified minimum.

- *max*: The max attribute sets the maximum time that the input field can accept. Users cannot select a time later than the specified maximum.

- *step*: The step attribute defines the increment or decrement step for the time input. It controls the granularity of the available time options. For example, step="15" represents 15-minute intervals, step="30" represents 30-minute intervals, and so on.

- *required*: The required attribute, when present, makes the time input a required field, meaning that users must select a time before submitting the form.

Datetime Input

The input element with type="datetime-local" is used to create a datetime input field in web forms. This input type is specifically designed for collecting date and time values from users, allowing them to choose both the date and time using a date and time picker.

Here's the basic syntax of the datetime input:

```
<input type="datetime-local" name="datetimeField"
id="datetimeFieldID">
```

Let's explore the attributes and characteristics of the datetime input:

- *type="datetime-local"*: This attribute specifies the type of the input element, which, in this case, is datetime-local.

- *name*: The name attribute is used to define a name for the input element. It is essential for form submission, as it identifies the input field and its associated value in the form data.

- *id*: The id attribute provides a unique identifier for the input element, allowing you to associate labels with the input using the for attribute.

- *value*: The value attribute sets the initial value of the input field. It should be in the format "YYYY-MM-DDTHH:mm," representing the date and time in year-month-day and hour-minute format.

- *min*: The min attribute sets the minimum datetime that the input field can accept. Users cannot select a datetime earlier than the specified minimum.

- *max*: The max attribute sets the maximum datetime that the input field can accept. Users cannot select a datetime later than the specified maximum.

- *step*: The step attribute defines the increment or decrement step for the datetime input. It controls the granularity of the available datetime options. For example, step="300" represents 5-minute intervals, step="1800" represents 30-minute intervals, and so on.

- *required*: The required attribute, when present, makes the datetime input a required field, meaning that users must select a date and time before submitting the form.

Month Input

The input element with type="month" is used to create a month input field in web forms. This input type is specifically designed for collecting month and year values from users, allowing them to choose a specific month and year using a month picker.

Here's the basic syntax of the month input:

```
<input type="month" name="monthField" id="monthFieldID">
```

Let's explore the attributes and characteristics of the month input:

- *type="month"*: This attribute specifies the type of the input element, which, in this case, is month.

- *name*: The name attribute is used to define a name for the input element. It is essential for form submission, as it identifies the input field and its associated value in the form data.

- *id*: The id attribute provides a unique identifier for the input element, allowing you to associate labels with the input using the for attribute.

- *value*: The value attribute sets the initial value of the input field. It should be in the format YYYY-MM, representing the year and month in year-month format.

- *min*: The min attribute sets the minimum month that the input field can accept. Users cannot select a month earlier than the specified minimum.

- *max*: The max attribute sets the maximum month that the input field can accept. Users cannot select a month later than the specified maximum.

- *step*: The step attribute defines the increment or decrement step for the month input. It controls the granularity of the available month options. For example, step="1" represents one month intervals, step="2" represents two-month intervals, and so on.

- *required*: The required attribute, when present, makes the month input a required field, meaning that users must select a month before submitting the form.

Week Input

The input element with type="week" is used to create a week input field in web forms. This input type is specifically designed for collecting week values from users, allowing them to choose a specific week using a week picker.

Here's the basic syntax of the week input:

```
<input type="week" name="weekField" id="weekFieldID">
```

Let's explore the attributes and characteristics of the week input:

- *type="week"*: This attribute specifies the type of the input element, which, in this case, is week.

- *name*: The name attribute is used to define a name for the input element. It is essential for form submission, as it identifies the input field and its associated value in the form data.

- *id*: The id attribute provides a unique identifier for the input element, allowing you to associate labels with the input using the for attribute.

- *value*: The value attribute sets the initial value of the input field. It should be in the format "YYYY-Www," representing the year and week in year-week format. The "Www" part represents the week number within the year.

- *min*: The min attribute sets the minimum week that the input field can accept. Users cannot select a week earlier than the specified minimum.

- *max*: The max attribute sets the maximum week that the input field can accept. Users cannot select a week later than the specified maximum.

- *step*: The step attribute defines the increment or decrement step for the week input. It controls the granularity of the available week options. For example, step="1" represents one-week intervals, step="2" represents two-week intervals, and so on.

- *required*: The required attribute, when present, makes the week input a required field, meaning that users must select a week before submitting the form.

Color Input

The input element with type="color" is used to create a color input field in web forms. This input type is specifically designed for collecting color values from users, allowing them to choose a specific color using a color picker.

Here's the basic syntax of the color input:

```
<input type="color" name="colorField" id="colorFieldID">
```

Let's explore the attributes and characteristics of the color input:

- *type="color"*: This attribute specifies the type of the input element, which, in this case, is color.

- *name*: The name attribute is used to define a name for the input element. It is essential for form submission, as it identifies the input field and its associated value in the form data.

- *id*: The id attribute provides a unique identifier for the input element, allowing you to associate labels with the input using the for attribute.

- *value*: The value attribute sets the initial value of the input field. It should be in the format "#RRGGBB" or "#RGB," representing the selected color in hexadecimal notation.

- *required*: The required attribute, when present, makes the color input a required field, meaning that users must select a color before submitting the form.

Checkbox Input

The input element with type="checkbox" is used to create a checkbox input field in web forms. This input type allows users to select one or multiple options from a set of choices.

Here's the basic syntax of the checkbox input:

```
<input type="checkbox" name="optionName" id="optionID"
value="optionValue">
```

Let's explore the attributes and characteristics of the checkbox input:

- *type="checkbox"*: This attribute specifies the type of the input element, which, in this case, is checkbox.

- *name*: The name attribute is used to define a name for the input element. It is essential for form submission, as it identifies the input field and its associated values in the form data. When multiple checkboxes have the same name, they will be treated as an array, allowing you to group them together and process their values more efficiently.

- *id*: The id attribute provides a unique identifier for the input element, allowing you to associate labels with the input using the for attribute.

- *value*: The value attribute sets the value that will be sent along with the form data when the checkbox is checked and the form is submitted. If this attribute is not provided, the default value of on will be sent.

- *checked*: The checked attribute, when present, makes the checkbox checked by default. If this attribute is omitted, the checkbox will initially be unchecked.

Radio Input

The input element with type="radio" is used to create a radio button input field in web forms. Radio buttons allow users to select one option from a group of mutually exclusive choices.

Here's the basic syntax of the radio input:

```
<input type="radio" name="groupName" id="optionID"
value="optionValue">
```

Let's explore the attributes and characteristics of the radio input:

- *type="radio"*: This attribute specifies the type of the input element, which, in this case, is radio.

- *name*: The name attribute is used to define a name for the input element. It is essential for form submission, as it identifies the input field and its associated value in the form data. All radio buttons that belong to the same group should have the same name, so they are treated as a single group of options.

- *id*: The id attribute provides a unique identifier for the input element, allowing you to associate labels with the input using the for attribute.

- *value*: The value attribute sets the value that will be sent along with the form data when the radio button is selected and the form is submitted. Each radio button in the same group should have a unique value to differentiate the selected option.

- *checked*: The checked attribute, when present, makes the radio button selected by default. However, only one radio button in a group should have the checked attribute, as radio buttons are mutually exclusive within a group.

File Input

The input element with type="file" is used to create a file input field in web forms. This input type allows users to browse their local file system and select one or multiple files to be uploaded to a server or processed by a client-side script.

Here's the basic syntax of the file input:

```
<input type="file" name="fileField" id="fileFieldID"
accept="fileType">
```

Let's explore the attributes and characteristics of the file input:

- *type="file"*: This attribute specifies the type of the input element, which, in this case, is file.

- *name*: The name attribute is used to define a name for the input element. It is essential for form submission, as it identifies the input field and its associated files in the form data.

- *id*: The id attribute provides a unique identifier for the input element, allowing you to associate labels with the input using the for attribute.

- *accept*: The accept attribute specifies the types of files that the file input should accept. It can be a comma-separated list of MIME types, file extensions, or a combination of both. For example, accept=".jpg,.png,image/jpeg,image/png" would allow the user to select only JPEG and PNG image files.

- *multiple*: The multiple attribute, when present, allows the user to select multiple files simultaneously. This attribute is optional, and if not provided, the user can select only one file at a time.

Search Input

The input element with type="search" is used to create a search input field in web forms. This input type is specifically designed for capturing search queries from users, and it typically provides a specialized appearance with a search icon or magnifying glass.

Here's the basic syntax of the search input:

```
<input type="search" name="searchField" id="searchFieldID"
placeholder="Search...">
```

Let's explore the attributes and characteristics of the search input:

- *type="search"*: This attribute specifies the type of the input element, which, in this case, is search.

- *name*: The name attribute is used to define a name for the input element. It is essential for form submission, as it identifies the input field and its associated value in the form data.

- *id*: The id attribute provides a unique identifier for the input element, allowing you to associate labels with the input using the for attribute.

- *placeholder*: The placeholder attribute is used to display a short hint inside the search input field when it is empty. It provides guidance to users on what type of information to enter, such as "Search...."

- *value*: The value attribute sets the initial value of the input field. Users can edit this value, and it will be submitted along with the form data.

- *autocomplete*: The autocomplete attribute indicates whether the browser should automatically complete the input based on the user's past entries. For search inputs, the default value is usually set to off to prevent suggestions based on previous searches.

Range Input

The input element with type="range" is used to create a range input slider in web forms. This input type allows users to select a value from a specified range by dragging a slider handle along a track.

Here's the basic syntax of the range input:

```
<input type="range" name="rangeField" id="rangeFieldID"
min="minValue" max="maxValue" step="stepValue"
value="defaultValue">
```

Let's explore the attributes and characteristics of the range input:

- *type–"range"*: This attribute specifies the type of the input element, which, in this case, is range.

- *name*: The name attribute is used to define a name for the input element. It is essential for form submission, as it identifies the input field and its associated value in the form data.

- *id*: The id attribute provides a unique identifier for the input element, allowing you to associate labels with the input using the for attribute.

- *min*: The min attribute sets the minimum value of the range. Users cannot select a value lower than the specified minimum.

- *max*: The max attribute sets the maximum value of the range. Users cannot select a value higher than the specified maximum.

- *step*: The step attribute defines the increment or decrement step for the range input. It controls the granularity of the available values. For example, step="1" allows only integer values, while step="0.1" allows decimal values with one decimal place.

- *value*: The value attribute sets the initial value of the range input. Users can interact with the slider to change the value, and it will be submitted along with the form data.

Submit Input

The input element with type="submit" is used to create a submit button in web forms. The submit button is used to trigger the submission of a form to a server for processing or to initiate some other action associated with the form.

Here's the basic syntax of the submit input:

```
<input type="submit" value="Submit Form">
```

Let's explore the attributes and characteristics of the submit input:

- *type="submit"*: This attribute specifies the type of the input element, which, in this case, is submit. When the user clicks a submit button, it signals the form to be submitted, sending its data to the server specified in the action attribute of the form element.

- *value*: The value attribute sets the text that appears on the submit button. It defines the label or display text that users see on the button.

Reset Input

The input element with type="reset" is used to create a reset button in web forms. The reset button is used to clear the user's input and restore the form's fields to their default values defined in the HTML markup.

Here's the basic syntax of the reset input:

```
<input type="reset" value="Reset Form">
```

Let's explore the attributes and characteristics of the reset input:

- *type="reset"*: This attribute specifies the type of the input element, which, in this case, is reset. When the user clicks a reset button, it resets all form fields to their initial values as defined in the HTML markup.

- *value*: The value attribute sets the text that appears on the reset button. It defines the label or display text that users see on the button.

Button Input

The input element with type="button" is used to create a generic button in web pages. Unlike the submit and reset buttons, the button input type does not have any inherent default behavior related to form submissions. Instead, it is primarily used to trigger custom JavaScript functions or perform other non-form-related actions.

Here's the basic syntax of the button input:

```
<input type="button" value="Click Me" onclick="myFunction()">
```

Let's explore the attributes and characteristics of the button input:

- *type="button"*: This attribute specifies the type of the input element, which, in this case, is button. Unlike submit and reset buttons, the button type does not trigger form submissions automatically.

- *value*: The value attribute sets the text that appears on the button. It defines the label or display text that users see on the button.

- *onclick*: The onclick attribute is used to define a JavaScript function that will be executed when the button is clicked. You can use this attribute to define custom actions or interactions associated with the button.

Polyfill Nonsupportive Browsers

Polyfilling in HTML5 refers to the practice of adding JavaScript code to provide support for HTML5 features in browsers that do not natively support them. This ensures a more consistent user experience across different browsers. Here's how you can polyfill nonsupportive browsers in HTML5:

1. *Identify the feature*: Identify the HTML5 feature that you want to polyfill. For example, it could be form validation, new input types, or other advanced form elements.

2. *Check browser support*: Check if the feature is supported natively by the target browsers you want to polyfill. You can use websites such as caniuse.com to check for feature support in various browsers.

3. *Select a polyfill*: Once you've identified the feature and checked browser support, find a suitable polyfill library that provides support for the feature in nonsupportive browsers. Popular polyfill libraries include Modernizr and Polyfill.io.

4. *Include the polyfill*: Add a reference to the polyfill library in your HTML file, typically in the <head> section, before any other scripts that rely on the polyfilled feature. You can use a CDN or host the library locally.

```
<!DOCTYPE html>
<html>
<head>
  <!-- Add the polyfill library -->
  <script src="path/to/polyfill-library.js"></script>
  <!-- Other head elements go here -->
</head>
<body>
  <!-- Your content here -->
</body>
</html>
```

5. *Initialize the polyfill*: Some polyfill libraries require you to explicitly initialize them. Follow the library's documentation to properly initialize the polyfill for the feature you want to support.

6. *Test and verify*: Test your web page in different browsers, including those that don't natively support the HTML5 feature. Ensure that the polyfill is working correctly and providing the expected behavior.

241

Keep in mind that not all HTML5 features can be perfectly polyfilled, and the performance and behavior may not be identical to native support. It's essential to choose reputable and well-maintained polyfill libraries and regularly update them to address any bugs or security issues. Additionally, as browsers evolve and gain more native support, you might eventually phase out some polyfills in favor of native support.

Summary

This chapter explained HTML form elements, how to create a form using HTML tags, and how to validate these fields. It covered the new form elements along with the existing ones as well as accessibility considerations and how these forms work on mobile devices. Additionally, the chapter covered how the newer form elements work with older browser versions and whether one should choose to provide this support or opt out of it.

CHAPTER 9

Cross-Browser Challenges and How to Resolve Them

This chapter covers cross-browser challenges and approaches for solving them. We'll cover progressive enhancement versus graceful degradation and help you choose the best approach for the situation. The chapter also covers Modernizr and how to use it in responsive design. Finally, we cover media query capabilities for Internet Explorer 6, 7, and 8.

Cross-Browser Challenges

In the ever-evolving landscape of web design, crafting seamless user experiences across a multitude of devices and screen sizes has become paramount. Responsive design strategies play a pivotal role in achieving this goal, ensuring that websites adapt gracefully to various contexts. Two prominent approaches in this realm are *progressive enhancement* and *graceful degradation*. Although these terms might sound similar, they embody distinct philosophies, each with its own set of principles and implications. This section delves into the fundamental differences between progressive enhancement and graceful degradation, shedding light on their significance in the realm of responsive design.

© Varun Gor 2023
V. Gor, *Creating Responsive Websites Using HTML5 and CSS3*,
https://doi.org/10.1007/978-1-4842-9783-4_9

Progressive Enhancement: Building from the Ground Up

Progressive enhancement is a design methodology that centers around starting with a core experience and gradually enhancing it as the user's device and capabilities permit. This approach focuses on delivering a baseline experience that functions across a wide array of devices, including older browsers and devices with limited capabilities. As the user's environment becomes more sophisticated, additional features and functionalities are introduced to enhance the user experience.

The following are the key principles of progressive enhancement:

- *Core functionality*: Progressive enhancement prioritizes delivering essential content and functionality to all users, regardless of their device's capabilities. This ensures that even basic devices can access the core purpose of a website.

- *Layered enhancement*: Developers build successive layers of enhancements, each adding new features or improvements. This method ensures that more advanced devices can take full advantage of the website's capabilities while still allowing basic devices to access its content.

- *Graceful adaptation*: Progressive enhancement promotes a graceful adaptation to varying user contexts by avoiding a one-size-fits-all approach. It recognizes that users have diverse needs and devices and tailors the experience accordingly.

Graceful Degradation: Starting at the Pinnacle

Graceful degradation, on the other hand, takes a somewhat different approach. It begins by designing a feature-rich experience optimized for the most advanced devices and browsers. As the user's context becomes less capable—because of factors such as outdated browsers or limited resources—elements of the design may be removed or simplified to ensure compatibility.

The following are the key principles of graceful degradation:

- *High-end design*: Graceful degradation prioritizes designing for the most advanced and capable devices, providing users with a visually appealing and feature-rich experience.

- *Feature removal*: As the user's context downgrades, elements that may hinder performance or compatibility are removed or scaled back. This ensures that the core functionality remains intact, even on less capable devices.

- *Risk of disruption*: Graceful degradation carries the risk of a suboptimal user experience if elements are not carefully removed or modified. Users with older devices may encounter usability issues or broken features.

Balancing Act: Which Approach to Choose?

The choice between progressive enhancement and graceful degradation depends on the project's objectives, target audience, and developer's philosophy. Both approaches have their merits and challenges, and understanding the context in which each is appropriate is crucial.

- *Progressive enhancement for inclusivity*: If inclusivity, accessibility, and broader device compatibility are paramount, progressive enhancement is the more suitable choice. It ensures that core content is accessible to a wide range of users, regardless of their device's capabilities.

- *Graceful degradation for visual appeal*: When aesthetics and high-end user experiences are the primary focus, graceful degradation can be preferred. This approach allows designers to create visually stunning websites optimized for modern devices, while still aiming to maintain core functionality on less advanced platforms.

In the realm of responsive design, progressive enhancement and graceful degradation stand as two distinct strategies, each with its own set of principles and implications. Progressive enhancement builds a solid foundation and progressively adds enhancements based on user capabilities, fostering inclusivity and adaptability. Graceful degradation starts with a feature-rich design and simplifies as the user's context downgrades, prioritizing aesthetics and advanced user experiences. Choosing the right approach depends on the project's goals and the desired balance between inclusivity and visual appeal. By understanding the fundamental differences between these strategies, designers and developers can make informed decisions that lead to more effective and user-friendly responsive designs.

Progressive Enhancement vs. Graceful Degradation

In the dynamic world of web design, crafting a seamless and engaging user experience across various devices has become a fundamental objective. As responsive design continues to evolve, designers are faced with a pivotal decision: whether to employ the principles of progressive enhancement or graceful degradation. Both approaches offer unique perspectives on how to achieve responsive design excellence, each catering to different priorities and contexts. This section delves into the strategic considerations behind selecting either progressive enhancement or graceful degradation, helping designers make informed decisions to best suit their project goals.

When to Choose Progressive Enhancement

Progressive enhancement is a philosophy rooted in ensuring that all users, regardless of their device's capabilities, can access core content and functionality. This approach starts with a basic, foundational experience that is accessible to even the simplest devices and gradually enhances it as the user's context allows. Progressive enhancement embodies the spirit of inclusivity and accessibility, making it a compelling choice for many design scenarios.

Here are the reasons for when you'd choose progressive enhancement:

- *Diverse audience*: If your target audience spans a wide range of devices, browsers, and technological capabilities, progressive enhancement is a prudent choice. It ensures that everyone can access the core content and functionality, promoting inclusivity.

- *Content focus*: When your primary objective is delivering content and functionality, rather than visual flair, progressive enhancement is highly effective. It centers on the essential aspects of your website, providing a consistent experience to all users.

- *Future-proofing*: As new devices and technologies emerge, progressive enhancement is better positioned to adapt to these changes. The foundational core ensures that your website remains relevant and accessible over time.

When to Choose Graceful Degradation

Graceful degradation takes a different route by designing for advanced devices first and then simplifying or removing elements for less capable contexts. This approach prioritizes delivering a high-end user experience on modern devices while ensuring core functionality remains intact, even if some features are sacrificed on older or less capable platforms.

Here are the reasons for when you'd choose graceful degradation:

- *Aesthetics and innovation*: If your project places a strong emphasis on visual appeal, aesthetics, and innovative design, graceful degradation can help you create an impressive user experience for modern devices. This approach allows you to fully leverage the capabilities of advanced technologies.

- *Feature-rich design*: When your goal is to provide a rich and immersive experience to users with modern devices, graceful degradation lets you build sophisticated features and interactions that might be resource-intensive or demanding.

- *Client expectations*: In scenarios where clients prioritize cutting-edge design and brand representation, graceful degradation can align with their expectations by delivering a superior experience on flagship devices.

Making the Choice: Balancing Priorities

Selecting the appropriate approach—progressive enhancement or graceful degradation—entails a comprehensive evaluation of your project's objectives, target audience, and design philosophy. Striking the right balance between inclusivity, accessibility, aesthetics, and innovation is crucial.

Consider the following factors to guide your decision:

- *Project goals*: Define whether the primary focus is content delivery, inclusivity, or high-end design.

- *Target audience*: Analyze your user base to determine their devices, browsers, and preferences.

- *Client expectations*: Align with client preferences and project requirements, especially when aesthetics play a significant role.

- *Future adaptability*: Anticipate how your chosen approach will stand the test of time and evolving technologies.

The choice between progressive enhancement and graceful degradation in responsive design hinges on a nuanced understanding of project goals and user expectations. Both approaches carry distinct advantages and challenges, catering to different aspects of design strategy. By meticulously evaluating the needs of your project and the desires of your audience, you can make an informed decision that results in a responsive design strategy aligned with your vision and objectives. Whether you opt for inclusivity and adaptability through progressive enhancement or embrace visual innovation with graceful degradation, the ultimate goal remains the same: to create exceptional user experiences across an array of devices.

Accommodating Older Versions of Internet Explorer

Do you need to accommodate older versions of Internet Explorer? There are two points to consider here. One is the current usage of Internet Explorer, and the second is how much effort it would require to fix the issues of HTML5 and CSS3 to make your website work on older versions of Internet Explorer.

Internet Explorer (IE) was big in the 1990s. As technology advanced, the usage of IE declined. The current usage of IE is about 1.13 percent compared to other modern browsers. The successor of Internet Explorer, which is Edge, is being used by 2.97 percent of the web audience.

A fix is certainly possible by polyfilling the majority of HTML5 and CSS3 features for older versions of Internet Explorer. The side effect of polyfilling is that it makes the website heavy on JavaScript code, and since this JavaScript code is specific to HTML5, it renders itself useless when it comes to code reusability. Additionally, the visual effect of rendering the page with polyfilling would not be as same as it is with the latest versions of browsers. Also, the development time to fix these new features would add on to the cost of developing the website.

Modernizr and How It Is Used in Responsive Design

In the rapidly evolving landscape of web development, staying current with the latest technologies and techniques is paramount. One of the fundamental challenges faced by web developers is ensuring that websites look and function properly across a wide range of devices and screen sizes. This is where Modernizr comes into play. Modernizr is a powerful JavaScript library that enables developers to detect the presence of specific HTML5 and CSS3 features in a user's browser. This information can then be used to tailor the website's design and functionality, making it an invaluable tool in the realm of responsive design.

What Is Modernizr?

Modernizr is an open-source JavaScript library that simplifies the process of detecting the availability of specific web technologies in a user's browser. These technologies often include HTML5 and CSS3 features that have varying levels of support across different browsers. By checking for the presence of these features, developers can determine whether certain design or functionality elements are supported, allowing them to provide graceful fallbacks or alternative solutions for older or less capable browsers.

Why Is Modernizr Important for Responsive Design?

Responsive design aims to create websites that adapt seamlessly to various screen sizes, from large desktop monitors to mobile phones. To achieve this, developers often rely on CSS media queries to apply different styles based on screen dimensions. However, the effectiveness of these media queries relies on the browser's understanding of certain CSS3 properties.

For example, if a developer is using a CSS3 property like border-radius to create rounded corners on elements, they need to ensure that this property is supported by the user's browser. If it's not supported, the design might break or appear differently than intended. This is where Modernizr steps in. By detecting whether the browser supports border-radius, developers can apply alternative styling using traditional methods if necessary, ensuring a consistent user experience across devices.

251

Using Modernizr in Responsive Design

Let's delve into some code examples to understand how Modernizr is used in responsive design scenarios.

- **Checking for CSS3 media queries support**

    Modernizr can detect if the browser supports CSS3 media queries. This is crucial for applying responsive styles based on screen dimensions.

    Here is the HTML:

```
<!DOCTYPE html>
<html>
<head>
  <title>Modernizr Example</title>
  <script src="modernizr.js"></script>
</head>
<body>
  <div id="content">
    <!-- Content goes here -->
  </div>
  <script>
    if (Modernizr.mq('only all')) {
      // Apply responsive styles here
    } else {
      // Provide fallback styles for older browsers
    }
  </script>
</body>
</html>
```

- **Feature detection for CSS transitions**

CSS transitions can enhance user experience by adding smooth animations to elements. However, not all browsers support this feature.

Here is the HTML:

```
<!DOCTYPE html>
<html>
<head>
  <title>Modernizr Example</title>
  <script src="modernizr.js"></script>
  <style>
    .box {
      width: 100px;
      height: 100px;
      background-color: #3498db;
      transition: background-color 0.3s;
    }
    .box:hover {
      background-color: #e74c3c;
    }
  </style>
</head>
<body>
  <div class="box"></div>
  <script>
    if (Modernizr.csstransitions) {
      // Browser supports CSS transitions, enable
      animations
    } else {
```

```
        // Provide alternative experience for older
        browsers
      }
    </script>
  </body>
</html>
```

Modernizr plays a pivotal role in modern web development, particularly in the context of responsive design. By allowing developers to detect the presence of specific HTML5 and CSS3 features, it empowers them to build websites that gracefully adapt to a wide range of devices and browsers. This results in a more consistent and enjoyable user experience, regardless of the user's chosen platform. As web technologies continue to evolve, tools like Modernizr will remain crucial to ensuring the compatibility and responsiveness of websites across various devices.

Modernizr and Its Support for HTML5

In the dynamic landscape of web development, staying up-to-date with the latest technologies and ensuring cross-browser compatibility is crucial. HTML5, the most recent version of the Hypertext Markup Language, has brought numerous enhancements to the web development ecosystem. However, not all browsers fully support every HTML5 feature. This is where Modernizr, a powerful JavaScript library, comes into play. In this section, we'll delve into Modernizr's support for HTML5 feature detection and how it contributes to creating robust and responsive web experiences.

Understanding Modernizr: A Brief Overview

By providing information on a user's browser, developers can adapt their code to gracefully degrade or provide alternatives for older or less capable browsers. This allows them to ensure a consistent user experience across various devices and browsers.

HTML5: The Evolution of Web Standards

HTML5 has revolutionized web development by introducing a plethora of new elements, attributes, and APIs that enable developers to create more interactive and semantically meaningful web content. Features such as <canvas>, <video>, <audio>, <localStorage>, and many more have significantly enhanced the possibilities of what can be achieved on the Web.

Modernizr and HTML5 Feature Detection

Modernizr's primary role is to perform feature detection, which involves checking whether a specific HTML5 feature is supported by the user's browser. This information is crucial for making informed decisions about how to render content or provide alternative solutions. Let's explore a few examples of how Modernizr can be used for HTML5 feature detection.

- **Checking for <video> element support**

  The <video> element is a cornerstone of HTML5, allowing seamless integration of videos into web content. However, browser support for video formats can vary.

Here is the HTML:

```
<!DOCTYPE html>
<html>
<head>
  <title>Modernizr Video Example</title>
  <script src="modernizr.js"></script>
</head>
<body>
  <div id="video-container">
    <video controls>
      <source src="example.mp4" type="video/mp4">
      <p>Your browser does not support the video
      tag.</p>
    </video>
  </div>
  <script>
    if (Modernizr.video) {
      // Browser supports HTML5 video
    } else {
      // Provide alternative content or instructions
    }
  </script>
</body>

</html>
```

- **Detecting <canvas> element support**

  The <canvas> element enables dynamic graphics and animations, but not all browsers fully support it.

Here is the HTML:

```html
<!DOCTYPE html>
<html>
<head>
  <title>Modernizr Canvas Example</title>
  <script src="modernizr.js"></script>
</head>
<body>
  <div id="canvas-container">
    <canvas id="myCanvas"></canvas>
  </div>
  <script>
    if (Modernizr.canvas) {
      var canvas = document.getElementById("myCanvas");
      // Start drawing on the canvas
    } else {
      // Provide alternative content or instructions
    }
  </script>
</body>
</html>
```

Modernizr plays a pivotal role in the world of web development, particularly in HTML5 feature detection. By allowing developers to ascertain whether specific HTML5 features are supported by a user's browser, Modernizr empowers them to create web experiences that gracefully adapt to various environments. This results in a consistent and user-friendly browsing experience across different devices and browsers. As the Web continues to evolve, Modernizr's role in enhancing cross-browser compatibility and ensuring the smooth integration of HTML5 features remains as important as ever.

Adding Media Query Capabilities for Internet Explorer 6, 7, and 8

Internet Explorer 6, 7, and 8 were once widely used browsers, but they lacked support for many modern CSS features, making responsive design a challenge. To address this, Modernizr, a feature detection library, comes to the rescue. In this section, we'll explore how to use Modernizr to handle min/max media capabilities for these older versions of Internet Explorer, ensuring a more consistent and functional experience for users.

Understanding the Problem: Limited Media Query Support

Internet Explorer 6, 7, and 8 were notorious for their limited support of CSS media queries, which are essential for responsive design. These browsers didn't understand media queries based on the min-width and max-width properties, making it challenging to create responsive layouts.

Introducing Modernizr's Feature Detection

Modernizr's feature detection allows us to determine the capabilities of a browser before applying certain CSS styles or JavaScript functionalities. In the context of min/max media queries, Modernizr can help us provide alternative styles or scripts if a browser doesn't support these queries.

Using Modernizr for Min/Max Media Queries

Let's consider an example of using Modernizr to apply different styles based on screen size for Internet Explorer 6, 7, and 8.

Here is the HTML:

```
<!DOCTYPE html>
<html>
<head>
  <title>Modernizr Min/Max Media Example</title>
  <script src="modernizr.js"></script>
  <style>
    .container {
      width: 100%;
      background-color: #f2f2f2;
    }
    .box {
      width: 50%;
      height: 200px;
      background-color: #3498db;
      margin: 0 auto;
    }

    /* Alternative styles for IE 6, 7, and 8 */
    .lt-ie9 .box {
      width: 100%;
      background-color: #e74c3c;
    }
  </style>
</head>
<body>
  <div class="container">
    <div class="box"></div>
  </div>
</body>
</html>
```

In this example, the .lt-ie9 class targets Internet Explorer versions 6, 7, and 8. If Modernizr detects that the browser supports media queries, the default styles will be applied. If not, the alternative styles for older browsers will take effect.

Modernizr is a powerful tool that enables developers to create more inclusive and responsive web designs, even for older and less capable browsers like Internet Explorer 6, 7, and 8. By leveraging Modernizr's feature detection capabilities, developers can apply alternative styles or scripts based on a browser's capabilities, ensuring that users on older browsers still have a functional and visually appealing experience. As we continue to embrace newer web technologies, Modernizr's role in enhancing cross-browser compatibility remains essential.

Conditional Loading with Modernizr

In the world of web development, ensuring that your website works seamlessly across various browsers and devices is a significant challenge. Different browsers have varying levels of support for HTML, CSS, and JavaScript features. Conditional loading is a technique used to load specific code or assets only when needed, based on the capabilities of the user's browser. Modernizr, a feature detection library, plays a crucial role in enabling conditional loading to enhance cross-browser compatibility. In this article, we'll delve into the concept of conditional loading using Modernizr and explore how it can improve the user experience.

Understanding Conditional Loading

Conditional loading involves serving different resources or code to different users based on specific conditions. In the context of web development, this usually means delivering alternative code or assets to users with older browsers that lack support for modern features. This technique is especially relevant when dealing with browsers such as Internet Explorer 6, 7, and 8, which have limited support for newer web technologies.

The Role of Modernizr

Modernizr is a JavaScript library that helps detect the capabilities of a user's browser by testing whether it supports specific HTML, CSS, and JavaScript features. This feature detection capability makes Modernizr an invaluable tool for implementing conditional loading.

Advantages of Conditional Loading with Modernizr

These are the advantages:

- *Improved performance*: Loading unnecessary code or assets can slow down a website's performance. With conditional loading, you load only what's necessary for a particular user, leading to faster load times.

- *Enhanced compatibility*: By delivering fallback code to browsers that lack support for certain features, you ensure a consistent user experience across all devices and browsers.

- *Reduced maintenance*: Rather than creating separate versions of your site for different browsers, you can maintain a single codebase and use conditional loading to address compatibility issues.

Implementing Conditional Loading with Modernizr

Let's consider an example of how to implement conditional loading using Modernizr. Suppose you want to load a different stylesheet for browsers that don't support CSS Grid layout.

Here is the HTML:

```
<!DOCTYPE html>
<html>
<head>
  <title>Conditional Loading with Modernizr</title>
  <script src="modernizr.js"></script>
  <link rel="stylesheet" href="styles.css">
  <script>
    if (!Modernizr.cssgrid) {
      var link = document.createElement('link');
      link.rel = 'stylesheet';
      link.href = 'fallback-styles.css';
      document.head.appendChild(link);
    }
  </script>
</head>
<body>
  <!-- Your website content here -->
</body>
</html>
```

In this example, the Modernizr.cssgrid condition checks if the browser supports CSS Grid layout. If it doesn't, a new <link> element is dynamically created and added to the <head> to load the fallback stylesheet fallback-styles.css.

Conditional loading with Modernizr is a powerful technique that allows developers to provide optimized experiences for users across a wide range of browsers. By detecting a browser's capabilities and loading appropriate resources accordingly, web developers can enhance performance, ensure compatibility, and reduce the need for maintaining multiple versions of a website. Modernizr's feature detection capability empowers developers to implement this technique effectively and create web experiences that cater to the unique requirements of various users.

Summary

This chapter discussed the challenges faced with responsive design to make it work across various range of browsers. We looked at progressive enhancement versus graceful degradation. The chapter also covered Modernizr and how it is used in responsive design. Adding media query support for older Internet Explorer version was covered as part of this chapter along with conditional loading with Modernizr.

Index

Printed in the United States
by Baker & Taylor Publisher Services